AF326702

Systematic Theology Workbook for Kids

Fun Bible Activities to Help Kids Understand God, Faith, and the Christian Life

TABLE OF CONTENTS

INTRODUCTION
GET READY TO KNOW GOD

Welcome to a very big adventure! You are about to start a project that is more exciting than building a giant LEGO castle or winning a soccer game. You are going to learn about the Person who made the stars, the oceans, and you.

The Bible tells us something amazing in **2 Peter 3:18**. It says, **"But grow in the grace and knowledge of our Lord and Savior Jesus Christ."** This means that God does not want to be a mystery to you. He wants you to know Him. He wants you to grasp how much He loves you and see the plan He has for the whole world.

This workbook is your guide to getting that knowledge. It is not a dry school book. It is a tool to help you see the big picture of faith. By the time you finish the last page, you will see how every story in the Bible fits together.

What is Systematic Theology?

That is a very long phrase, isn't it? Do not let the big words worry you. Let's break it down into two simple parts.

Theology simply means "the study of God." Every time you think about God or ask a question about the Bible, you are doing theology. If you wonder why God made the world or how Jesus could walk on water, you are a mini-theologian!

Systematic means "organized" or "put into a system." Think about your favorite grocery store. Imagine if the manager just threw all the food into one big pile in the middle of the store. You would find a gallon of milk sitting on top of a pile of hammers. You would find frozen pizza mixed in with the bananas. It would take you hours to find what you need.

A good store is systematic. It puts the fruit in one section and the cereal in another. This makes it easy for you to find exactly what you want. **Systematic Theology** does the same thing with the Bible. The Bible is a big book with 66 different parts. It has stories, poems, and letters. Sometimes, it is hard to find everything the Bible says about a specific topic, like angels or heaven.

This book takes those big topics and groups them together. We call these groups "doctrines." In each chapter, we will gather the pieces of the puzzle. When we put them together, we see a clear image of who God is.

Why Do We Need This Book?

You might wonder why you can't just read the Bible from start to finish. You should definitely do that! But the Bible is like a massive ocean. Sometimes, it helps to have a map so you know where the deepest parts are.

This workbook helps you build a solid foundation. Imagine building a house on a pile of sand. When the wind blows and the rain falls, the house will fall down. But if you build your house on a solid rock, it stays still. Learning these truths is like building your life on a rock. When you have hard questions or face tough times, you will know what is true. You won't have to guess what God thinks about you. You will know because you studied His Word.

How This Workbook Works

Each chapter in this book is like a new level in a game. You will learn a new truth and then use your brain and your hands to make it stick. Here is what you will find in every chapter:

- **The Focus Verse:** We start with one specific verse. This verse is the "key" to the whole lesson. I want you to read it out loud. Maybe even write it on a sticky note and put it on your mirror. This is a direct quote from God to you.

- **The Big Truth:** Here, we explain the topic. We use simple words to talk about things like creation, sin, and grace. We focus on the facts. We look at what the Bible says is true, no matter how we feel that day.

- **Action Activities:** This is the fun part! You will find crosswords, secret codes, and drawing challenges. We also included some "Home Labs." These are simple science experiments or crafts you can do with things in your kitchen. These activities help you see the truth in real life.

- **A Simple Prayer:** We end every chapter by talking to God. Knowing things about God is good, but knowing God as a friend is better. Prayer is how we build that friendship.

The Tools You Need

Before you turn to Chapter 1, let's make sure your workspace is ready. You do not need a lot of gear, but a few things will help:

1. **A Bible:** This is the most important tool. This workbook points to the Bible, but it does not replace it. Use a version that is easy for you to read. The ESV or NIrV are great choices for your age.

2. **Pencils and Colored Markers:** You will be doing a lot of drawing and writing. Use bright colors! God made a colorful world, so your workbook should be colorful too.

3. **A Curious Mind:** Do not be afraid to ask "Why?" or "How?" God is big enough to handle your questions. If you find something hard to grasp, ask a parent or a teacher to talk about it with you.

4. **A Little Time:** You do not have to rush. You could do one chapter a week. Take your time to think about the verses. Let the truths sink into your heart.

Is This Book for You?

If you are between 8 and 12 years old, this book was written just for you. But it is also great to share! You can work through these pages with a best friend or a sibling. You can even bring it to your Sunday School class.

Maybe you have been going to church your whole life. Or maybe you just picked up a Bible for the first time yesterday. It does not matter! This book starts at the very beginning. We will talk about how we got the Bible, who Jesus is, and what happens at the end of time.

A Quick Note to the Grown-Ups

If you are a parent or teacher reading this with a child, thank you! You are doing a great job. Your goal is to help your child see that the Bible is a cohesive story. It is not just a bunch of random rules. It is a story of a King who loves His people.

Feel free to help with the activities. Some of the "Home Labs" might need an extra pair of hands. Most importantly, listen to the questions your child asks. You don't always need to have the perfect answer. Just searching for the answer together in the Bible is a great way to bond.

Let's Start the Search

God is the Creator of everything. He is the King of kings. He is also a Father who loves His children. Getting to know Him is the best way to spend your time. When you know who God is, you start to know who you are, too.

You were made for a purpose. You were made to know God and enjoy Him forever. This book is just the start of that lifelong relationship.

Are you ready? Grab your favorite pen. Open your Bible. Let's look into the Word of God and see what He has to say to us!

CHAPTER 1

TRUST THE WORD OF GOD

Imagine you are camping in a deep, dark forest. The sun has gone down, and you cannot see your own hand in front of your face. You need to find your way back to your tent, but every tree looks the same. Suddenly, someone hands you a powerful flashlight. With one click, the path appears. You can see the rocks, the roots, and the trail. You are safe because you have light.

The Bible is that flashlight for your life. Without it, we would just be guessing about who God is. We would not know how we got here or where we are going. But God did not leave us in the dark. He gave us a book.

"Your word is a lamp for my feet, a light on my path."
(Psalm 119:105)

Think about what a lamp does for your feet. It does not just show you the whole world at once. It shows you exactly where to step next. When you read the Bible, God shows you how to make good choices right now.

What is the Bible Exactly?

The Bible is not just one thick book. It is actually a library of 66 smaller books. It was written over a period of 1,600 years. That is a very long time! More than 40 different people wrote parts of it. Some were kings, some were fishermen, and one was even a doctor.

Even though many people wrote it, the Bible has only one main Author: God.

How does that work? The Bible explains this in a cool way. It says that all Scripture is "God-breathed." This does not mean God grew a pair of lungs and blew on the paper. It means His Spirit guided the writers. He made sure they wrote exactly what He wanted us to know. They used their own style and their own words, but the message came straight from God.

The Two Big Parts

The Bible is split into two main sections.

1. **The Old Testament:** This part was written before Jesus was born. It tells the story of how God made the world. It shows how He chose a special family (the Israelites) to show His love to the world. It is full of promises that a Savior was coming.

2. **The New Testament:** This part starts with the birth of Jesus. It tells us about His life, His death, and how He rose from the grave. It also tells us how the first churches started and how we can live for God today.

Both parts fit together like two pieces of a heart. You cannot have one without the other. The Old Testament promises the Savior, and the New Testament shows us who He is.

Why Can We Trust It?

Some people say the Bible is just a book of fairy tales. But that is not true. There are three big reasons we can trust every word:

- **History Matches Up:** People who dig in the dirt (archaeologists) have found cities, coins, and buildings mentioned in the Bible. Every time they find something new, it proves the Bible was right about history.

- **Prophecies Come True:** A prophecy is when God tells someone what will happen in the future. The Bible has hundreds of these. For example, prophets said exactly where Jesus would be born hundreds of years before it happened. He was born in Bethlehem, just like they said.

- **It Changes Lives:** Millions of people have read this book and found hope. It helps people stop being mean and start being kind. It gives peace to people who are scared. A book of lies cannot change a human heart, but the Word of God can.

Activity 1: The Scripture Map

A map helps you get from Point A to Point B. In the space below (or on a piece of paper), draw a map of your own life.

1. Draw a "Start" line where you were born.
2. Draw a "Current Spot" where you are right now.
3. Add "Roadblocks" for things that are hard for you (like a tough subject in school or a fight with a friend).
4. Pick three Bible verses and write them next to the "Roadblocks."

For example, if you are scared, write: *"When I am afraid, I put my trust in you"* (Psalm 56:3). Now, look at your map. See how God's Word acts like a light on your path? It gives you a way through the hard parts!

Activity 2: The Bible Library Word Search

The Bible is a library full of special words. Can you find these six words in the list below? Write them down or see if you can spot them in your own Bible.

- **SCRIPTURE:** A fancy name for the holy words found in the Bible.

- **TESTAMENT:** This is a "Big Promise" God made to His people.

- **GOSPEL:** This means "Great News!" It tells us all about Jesus.

- **PROPHET:** A messenger God chose to share His words with others.

- **PSALM:** A song or a poem written to praise God.

- **AUTHOR:** The person who writes a story. God is the main Author of the Bible!

Home Lab: The Invisible Ink Message

God's Word is sometimes hidden in our hearts. Try this to see how "hidden" things can become clear.

What you need:

- A lemon or a little bit of milk
- A cotton swab (Q-tip)
- A white piece of paper
- A desk lamp (with a bulb that gets warm)

What to do:

1. Dip the swab into the lemon juice or milk.
2. Write your favorite Bible verse on the paper. It will look like nothing is there when it dries.
3. Hold the paper close to a warm light bulb (ask a parent for help!).
4. Watch as the heat makes the words appear!

The Lesson: Sometimes we don't understand the Bible right away. But when we spend time with God and let His "light" shine on the words, the meaning becomes clear.

How to Read Your Bible

You do not have to read 50 pages a day. Just start small. Here are three tips for your daily Bible time:

1. **Pick a Book:** Start with the Book of Mark in the New Testament. It is fast and full of action.
2. **Ask a Question:** After you read a few verses, ask: "What does this tell me about God?"
3. **Talk to God:** Tell Him what you learned. If you don't understand something, tell Him that too!

Talk to God

Dear God, thank You for giving me a flashlight for my life. Thank You for the Bible. Help me to trust what it says, even when I have big questions. Show me how to use Your Word to make good choices today. Amen.

CHAPTER 2

MEET THE ONE TRUE CREATOR

Have you ever spent an afternoon building something amazing with blocks or craft supplies? Maybe you built a tall tower or a colorful birdhouse. When you finished, you probably felt proud. You looked at your work and saw your own ideas come to life. You knew every piece of that project because you were the one who put it together.

The world is God's giant project. When we look at a tall mountain, a tiny ladybug, or the vast blue ocean, we are looking at God's handiwork. But God did more than just leave us a beautiful world to look at. He gave us His name. He told us His story. He wants you to know exactly who He is.

In this chapter, we are going to learn about the character of God. This is the foundation of everything else we believe. If we don't know who God is, we won't understand why He does what He does. Let's look at the amazing truth of our Creator.

"I am the Lord, and there is no other; apart from me there is no God. I will strengthen you, though you have not acknowledged me." (Isaiah 45:5)

This verse is like a royal decree. It tells us that God does not have any rivals. There are not many gods fighting for control of the weather or the stars. There is only one King. He is the only one who deserves our worship. He is the Boss of everything because He made everything. He is the first, the last, and the only True God.

Who is God?

Imagine trying to describe the entire ocean to a friend who has only ever seen a glass of water. It would be very hard, wouldn't it? You would talk about the waves, the deep trenches, and the millions of fish. Even then, your friend might not truly grasp how big the ocean is.

God is much bigger than our brains can fully understand. However, God does not want to be a total mystery to us. He tells us exactly who He is in the Bible. He uses special traits called **attributes**. Attributes are things that are always true about Him.

Humans change all the time. You might be happy one minute and grumpy the next. You grow taller every year. You learn new things and forget old ones. But God does not change. He does not have "bad days" where He is less kind or less powerful. He is the same yesterday, today, and forever.

The Six Great Truths About God

Let's look at six big things that make God who He is. These are the things that set Him apart from every person, every angel, and every creature.

1. God is Eternal

Everything you see had a beginning. You had a birthday. Your parents had a birthday. Even the trees, the rocks, and the sun had a start date. But God never had a start. He was always there before time began.

Think of a circle. If you put your finger on a circle and follow the line, you can never find the spot where it starts or ends. God is like that. He is the "Alpha and Omega," which are the first and last letters of the Greek alphabet. He has always existed, and He will always exist. This means He is never in a hurry and He never runs out of time.

2. God is All-Powerful (Omnipotent)

Have you ever tried to lift something that was just too heavy? We all have limits. We get tired, we get sick, and we run out of strength. God has no limits.

The Bible says that God spoke, and the stars appeared. He didn't need tools or a factory. He just used His powerful word. **Omnipotent** is a big word that means "all-powerful." There is no problem too big for God to solve. There is no enemy too strong for Him to defeat. When you feel small or weak, you can remember that your Father is the strongest force in the universe.

3. God is Everywhere (Omnipresent)

If you are at school, you cannot be at home at the same time. If you are in the living room, you aren't in the kitchen. We can only be in one place at a time. But God is everywhere at once.

He is with you while you read this book. He is also with a child on the other side of the planet at the exact same moment. He is at the bottom of the deepest ocean and on the highest mountain peak. This is wonderful news because it means you are never truly alone. You never have to go searching for God. He is always close enough to hear your quietest whisper.

4. God Knows Everything (Omniscient)

Think about the smartest person you know. Maybe it is a teacher or a scientist. Even they have to study and learn new things. God never has to learn. He already knows everything that has ever happened and everything that will happen.

He knows how many hairs are on your head. He knows the names of every star in the sky. He even knows what you are going to say before the words come out of your mouth! You never have to explain your feelings to God because He already sees them. He knows your heart better than you do, and He still loves you perfectly.

5. God is Holy

The word **holy** means that God is completely "set apart." He is perfect in every way. He never makes a mistake. He never thinks a mean thought. He never tells a lie.

Imagine a light so bright that it makes everything else look dim. That is like God's holiness. Because He is holy, He cannot be around sin. He is like a perfect judge who always does what is right and fair. Knowing God is holy helps us understand why we need Him to lead us. We want to follow the One who is always right.

6. God is Love

This might be the most famous thing about God. The Bible does not just say that God *acts* in a loving way. It says that **God is love**. Everything He does comes from His goodness.

Even when God gives us rules to follow, He does it because He loves us. Think about a parent who tells a child not to touch a hot stove. That rule is not there to be mean. It is there to protect the child. God's love is even bigger than that. He loves us so much that He wants to be with us forever.

How Can We See God?

Since we cannot see God with our eyes right now, how do we know He is there? God shows Himself to us in two main ways.

Nature: The Fingerprint of God When you look at a beautiful sunset, you see God's love for color and beauty. When you see a thunderstorm, you see His power. This is called "General Revelation." It is like finding a footprint in the sand. You might not see the person, but you know someone was there. Nature tells every person on earth that there is a powerful and creative God.

The Bible: The Voice of God Nature tells us that God is powerful, but it doesn't tell us His name. It doesn't tell us how to be saved or how much He loves us. For that, we need the Bible. This is called "Special Revelation." In the Bible, God speaks directly to us. He tells us His promises. He shows us His heart. While nature shows us His "fingerprint," the Bible shows us His "face."

To complete this hunt, you need to look around your house or your yard. Find an object that reminds you of one of God's traits. Write down what you found and why it reminds you of Him.

1. **Something Strong:** (Example: A heavy rock or a thick tree branch).
   - *I found:* _______________________________________
   - *Why:* ____
2. **Something Light:** (Example: A flashlight or a candle).
   - *I found:* _______________________________________
   - *Why:* ____
3. **Something Heart-Shaped:** (Example: A leaf or a drawing).
   - *I found:* _______________________________________
   - *Why:* ____
4. **Something Old:** (Example: An old photo or an antique book).
   - *I found:* _______________________________________
   - *Why:* ____

Activity 2: Word Hunt – God's Character

The Bible uses many special words to describe God. Can you find these six words in your heart or write them down?

- **ETERNAL:** God has no beginning and no end.

   ____

   ____

- **HOLY:** God is perfect and pure.

   ____

   ____

- **POWERFUL:** God can do anything.

   ____

   ____

- **LOVE:** God cares for us deeply.

- **PRESENT:** God is always with us.

- **CREATOR:** God made everything from nothing.

Home Lab: The Stained Glass Reminder

God's character is beautiful. It is like light shining through colored glass. Each color represents a different trait of God, but they all come from the same light.

What you need:
- Black construction paper
- Tissue paper (different colors)
- Scissors and glue
- A window with bright sunlight

What to do:
1. Draw a large shape on your black paper, like a cross or a star.
2. Carefully cut out the middle of the shape so you only have a black outline.
3. Cut small squares of colorful tissue paper.
4. Glue the tissue paper over the hole in your black paper. Use different colors for different attributes! Blue for power, red for love, white for holiness.
5. Tape your "stained glass" to a sunny window.

The Lesson: When the sun shines through the paper, the colors glow. This reminds us that when we get to know God, His light shines through our lives. People can see His love and kindness in the way we act!

Think About This: God is Our Father

While God is the King of the Universe, He also uses a very personal name. He invites us to call Him **Father**.

This is amazing! The same God who created the galaxies wants to have a relationship with you. A good father listens when his children talk. A good father protects his children from danger. A good father provides what his children need.

God is the perfect Father. Even if you have a great dad on earth, God is even better. If you don't have a dad around, God promises to be a Father to you. He is never too busy to listen to your prayers. He never gets tired of your questions. You are His child, and He delights in you.

Talk to God

Dear God, thank You for being the one true Creator. You are so much bigger and better than I can imagine. Thank You for being powerful enough to protect me and kind enough to love me. Thank You for being my Heavenly Father. Help me to trust You more every day as I learn about who You are. Amen.

CHAPTER 3

SEE GOD IN THREE PERSONS

Have you ever looked at a fidget spinner or a three-leaf clover? These are simple things that have three distinct parts but are still just one object. Today, we are going to look at the biggest mystery in the whole Bible. It is a concept that has made even the smartest people in history scratch their heads.

This mystery is called the **Trinity**.

The word "Trinity" is not actually in the Bible, but the idea is on almost every page. It describes how God is one God, but He exists in three distinct persons: the Father, the Son, and the Holy Spirit. If that sounds a bit confusing, do not worry! It is supposed to be big. If we could explain God as easily as a math problem, He wouldn't be God.

The Focus Verse

"Therefore go and make disciples of all nations, baptizing them in the name of the Father and of the Son and of the Holy Spirit," (Matthew 28:19)

Notice something very important in this verse. Jesus does not say to baptize them in the "names" (plural). He says in the "name" (singular). This is a huge clue! There is one name, one God, but three Persons mentioned. All three are equal, and all three have been together forever.

The Math of God

In your math class, you know that $1 + 1 + 1 = 3$. That is how the world works. But when we talk about God, the math looks a little different. It is more like $1 \times 1 \times 1 = 1$.

The Father is God.

The Son (Jesus) is God.

The Holy Spirit is God.

But there are not three gods. There is only one. Think of a musical chord. When a piano player hits three different notes at the same time, it makes one beautiful sound. You can hear the individual notes if you listen closely, but they work together to make one harmony. That is a small way to think about the Trinity.

1. God the Father: The Planner

When we think of God the Father, we often think of the Creator. He is the one who spoke the world into existence. He is like the great architect of a building. He drew the plans for the universe and knows exactly how everything should work.

The Father is the one who sent Jesus to earth because He loves us so much. He is also the one we talk to when we pray "Our Father, who art in heaven." He cares for us, protects us, and has a perfect plan for our lives. He is the source of all life and the King over all creation.

2. God the Son: The Savior

The Son is Jesus Christ. A common mistake is thinking that Jesus only started existing when He was born as a baby in Bethlehem. That is not true! Jesus has always existed with the Father. He was there when the stars were made.

Jesus is the "Word made flesh." This means He is the part of God we can see and touch. He came to earth to show us exactly what God is like. If you want to know how God feels about people who are hurting, look at Jesus. If you want to know how God feels about sin, look at Jesus.

Jesus did something no one else could do. Because He is 100% God and 100% man, He could be the bridge between us and the Father. He lived a perfect life and then took the punishment for our mistakes on the cross. He is our King, our Brother, and our best Friend.

3. God the Spirit: The Helper

The Holy Spirit is the third person of the Trinity. Sometimes people think of the Spirit as a "force" or a "ghost," but He is a Person. He has feelings, He speaks, and He helps us.

Before Jesus went back to heaven, He promised to send a Helper. That Helper is the Holy Spirit. Today, the Spirit lives inside everyone who trusts in Jesus. He is like a built-in compass. He helps us know right from wrong. He gives us the strength to be kind when we feel like being mean. He also helps us grasp the words we read in the Bible. He is God's presence with us every single day.

Seeing the Trinity in Action

One of the best places to see the Trinity is at the baptism of Jesus. Imagine you are standing by the Jordan River. You see Jesus (the Son) come out of the water. Suddenly, the sky opens up. The Holy Spirit comes down from heaven looking like a gentle dove and rests on Jesus. Then, a loud voice from heaven (the Father) says, "This is my beloved Son, in whom I am well pleased."

In that one moment, all three Persons of the Trinity were right there!

- **The Son** was in the water.
- **The Spirit** was descending like a dove.
- **The Father** was speaking from heaven.

They were working together to show the world that Jesus was starting His special mission.

Activity 1: The Three-in-One Science Lab

This experiment helps you see how one thing can be three things at the same time.

What you need:

- An adult to help you
- An ice cube
- A pot of water
- A stove

What to do:

1. **Solid:** Look at the ice cube. It is hard and cold. It is water (H_2O).
2. **Liquid:** Put the ice cube in the pot and turn on the heat. Soon, it melts. Now it is liquid. It looks different, but it is still water (H_2O).
3. **Gas:** Keep the water boiling. Look at the steam rising from the pot. That is water vapor. It is invisible and moves through the air. It is still water (H_2O).

The Lesson: Water can be ice, liquid, or steam. It is always the same substance, but it shows up in three different ways. This is a tiny bit like how God is Father, Son, and Spirit.

Activity 2: The Trinity Clover Hunt

Go outside and look for a three-leaf clover (or a shamrock). If you can't find one, you can draw one on a piece of paper.

1. On the first leaf, write **FATHER**.
2. On the second leaf, write **SON**.
3. On the third leaf, write **SPIRIT**.
4. In the center where the leaves meet, write **GOD**.

Now, try to pull one leaf off without touching the center. It is hard to do! The leaves are separate, but they are all part of the same plant. This is a famous way people have explained the Trinity for hundreds of years.

Why Does the Trinity Matter?

You might think, "This is cool, but does it change how I live?" Yes, it does! Here are three reasons why the Trinity is important for you:

1. God is never lonely. Because God is a Trinity, He has always been in a relationship. Before the world was made, the Father, Son, and Spirit loved each other. This means God didn't create you because He was bored or lonely. He created you because He has so much love that He wanted to share it with you!

2. We have a perfect example of teamwork. The Father, Son, and Spirit always work together. They never argue. They never try to show off. They show us how to treat our friends and family. When we work together with others, we are acting like God.

3. We are fully covered. The Father planned your life. The Son saved your life. The Spirit guides your life. Every part of God is working to help you know Him. You aren't just following a distant King; you are being cared for by a Team that loves you perfectly.

Activity 3: The Secret Code Message

Use the key below to find out what the Bible says about our relationship with the Trinity.

A=1, B=2, C=3, D=4, E=5, F=6, G=7, H=8, I=9,
L=12, O=15, S=19, T=20, U=21, V=22, W=23

"7 - 15 - 4" (___ ___ ___)

"9 - 19" (___ ___)

"12 - 15 - 22 - 5" (___ ___ ___ ___)

The Answer: "God is Love."

Wait, how does that relate to the Trinity? Because to have "love," you need someone to give love and someone to receive love. Because God is three Persons, He has been loving for all of eternity!

"Is Jesus just a junior version of God?"

No way! Jesus is just as much God as the Father is. He has all the power and all the holiness of God. He just has a different role.

"If Jesus is God, who was He talking to when He prayed?"

This is a great question. When Jesus was on earth, He talked to God the Father. This shows us that the three Persons of the Trinity really are distinct. They can talk to each other and love each other.

"Can I see the Holy Spirit?"

Not with your eyes. The Bible compares the Spirit to the wind. You cannot see the wind, but you can see what the wind *does*. You can see the leaves move on a tree. In the same way, you can see the Spirit by the way He changes people's hearts and makes them more like Jesus.

Home Lab: The Trinity Pretzel

This is a tasty way to remember the lesson!

What you need:

- Pretzel dough or store-bought soft pretzels
- Salt
- A baking sheet

What to do:

1. Take a long piece of dough and roll it into a snake.
2. Cross the ends over to make three distinct loops that all join in the middle.
3. Bake them and enjoy!

The Lesson: As you eat your pretzel, look at the three loops. Each loop is separate, but they are all made of the same dough. They are joined together to make one snack. This is a reminder of our one God in three Persons.

Dear God, thank You for being so big that I cannot fully grasp everything about You. Thank You, Father, for making me. Thank You, Jesus, for saving me. Thank You, Holy Spirit, for being my Helper. I am glad that I can know You and that You are always with me. Help me to show Your love to others today. Amen.

CHAPTER 4

EXPLORE THE WORLD GOD MADE

Have you ever walked outside on a clear night and looked up at the stars? It feels like looking at a giant, sparkling blanket. Or have you ever watched a tiny ant carry a crumb three times its size? When we look at the world, we are seeing a masterpiece. Every mountain, every whale, and every atom was put there on purpose.

In the first three chapters, we learned about the Bible and who God is. Now, we are going to look at the first thing God did in the Bible. He created. He went from being the only thing that existed to being the King of a massive, colorful universe.

"In the beginning God created the heavens and the earth."
(Genesis 1:1)

This is the very first sentence of the Bible. It is short, but it tells us a lot. It tells us that time has a "start." It tells us that God was already there before the start. And it tells us that everything we see, the "heavens and the earth", belongs to Him because He made it.

The Big Start: Out of Nothing

When you build a birdhouse, you need wood, nails, and a hammer. You take things that already exist and put them together. God did something different. He created "ex nihilo." That is a Latin phrase that means "out of nothing."

Before God started, there was no dirt. There was no air. There was no light. There was only God. Then, God spoke. He didn't use a magic wand or a construction crew. His words have so much strength that when He said, "Let there be light," light appeared instantly.

The Seven Days of Creation

God is a God of order. He didn't just throw everything into a pile. He built the world like a beautiful house, room by room. Let's look at how He did it.

Day 1: Light and Dark

God created light. He separated the light from the darkness. This gave us day and night. Think about how fast light travels. It moves at 186,000 miles per second! God made that entire system with just one sentence.

Day 2: The Sky and Water

God made the atmosphere. He separated the water on the earth from the clouds in the sky. He gave us air to breathe and a beautiful blue sky to look at.

Day 3: Land and Plants

God told the water to move aside so dry land could appear. Then, He decorated the land. He made grass, trees, flowers, and fruit. He didn't just make one type of plant; He made thousands! He made prickly cacti, giant redwood trees, and sweet strawberries.

Day 4: Sun, Moon, and Stars

Wait a minute! God made light on Day 1, but He made the sun on Day 4? Yes! This shows that God is the source of all light. On Day 4, He put "lights" in the sky to help us track time, seasons, and years. The sun gives us warmth, the moon guides the tides, and the stars show us how vast God's imagination is.

Day 5: Birds and Fish

The sky and the oceans were ready for life. God made creatures to fly through the air and swim through the deep. He made the tiny hummingbird and the massive blue whale on the same day. He told them to fill the earth with even more life.

Day 6: Land Animals and Humans

This was a very busy day! God made lions, elephants, dogs, and bugs. But then, He did something extra special. He made humans. We will talk more about this in the next chapter, but for now, remember that humans are the "crown" of creation. We were made to rule over the earth and take care of it.

Day 7: Rest

Did God get tired? No! Remember, God never runs out of energy. He rested to show us a pattern. He stopped to enjoy what He had made. He looked at everything and said it was "very good."

Why Did God Create the World?

God didn't create the world because He was bored. He didn't need us to keep Him company. He created the world for two big reasons.

1. To Show His Glory The world is like a giant sign pointing to God. The thunder shows His power. The sunset shows His beauty. The way your body heals a paper cut shows His wisdom. Every part of nature says, "Look how amazing my Creator is!"

2. To Share His Love God is full of joy. He wanted to create beings who could enjoy the world with Him. He wanted us to see the stars and feel the wind and know that He is good. Creation is a gift from God to us.

Activity 1: The Creation Calendar

In the sections below (or on a separate paper), Draw a small icon or symbol for each day of creation. Use the list above to help you.

- **Day 1:** (Maybe a sunbeam or a candle)

- **Day 2:** (Maybe a cloud or a wave)

- **Day 3:** (Maybe a flower or a mountain)

- **Day 4:** (Maybe a crescent moon and stars)

- **Day 5:** (Maybe a bird wing or a fish tail)

- **Day 6:** (Maybe a paw print or a person)

- **Day 7:** (Maybe a pillow or a smiley face)

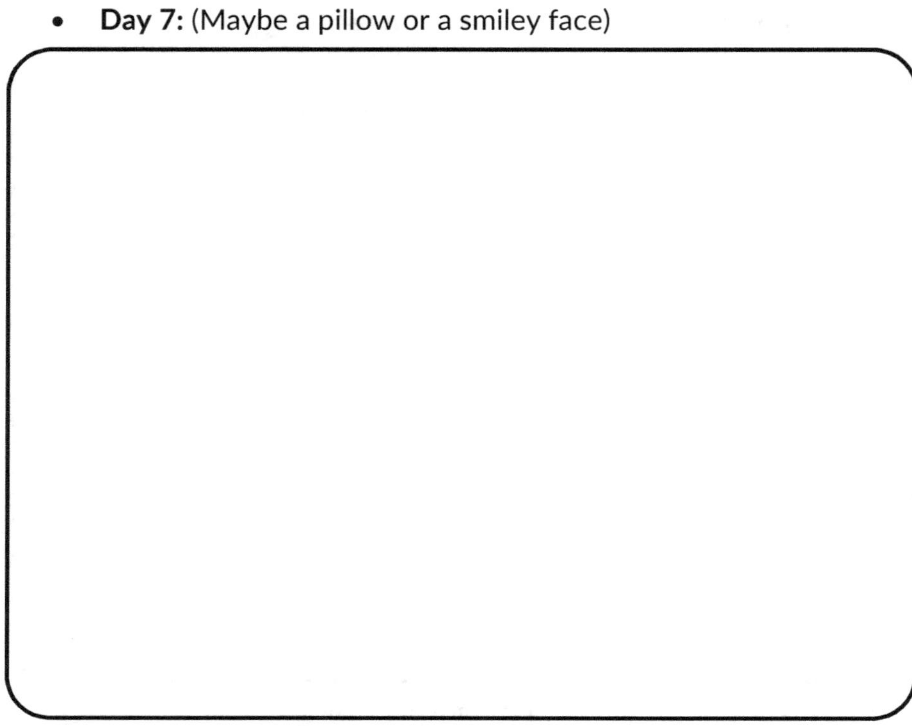

Once you finish, look at your calendar. Which day is your favorite? Why do you think God chose that specific order?

Activity 2: The Seven Days of Art

God used words to create, but He also used color and shape. You are an artist too! Pick one "Day" from the list. Get a piece of paper and use markers, paint, or crayons to make the most detailed version of that day you can imagine.

If you pick **Day 5**, don't just draw one fish. Draw a coral reef with neon fish, a shark, and a jellyfish! If you pick **Day 3**, draw a forest with different types of leaves. When you finish, show your art to someone and tell them what God created on that day.

Taking Care of the House

Since God made the world and gave it to us, we have a job to do. This job is called **stewardship**. A steward is someone who takes care of something that belongs to someone else.

Imagine your friend lets you borrow their favorite video game. You wouldn't throw it in the mud or break the case, right? You would keep it safe because it belongs to your friend. The earth belongs to God, but He let us "borrow" it.

We can be good stewards by:

- Not wasting water or food.
- Taking care of animals.
- Not littering in the park.
- Thanking God for the beautiful things we see.

Home Lab: The "Breath of Life" Seed Experiment

God gave plants the ability to grow from tiny seeds. You can watch this happen in your own kitchen!

What you need:

- A clear plastic bag
- A paper towel
- A few dried beans (like lima beans or kidney beans)
- A little water

What to do:

1. Wet the paper towel so it is damp but not dripping.
2. Fold the towel and put it inside the plastic bag.
3. Place the beans on top of the paper towel.
4. Seal the bag and tape it to a sunny window.
5. Check it every day for a week.

The Lesson: Within a few days, you will see a tiny sprout come out of the bean. This is the "life" God put inside every plant on Day 3. Even a tiny bean has a plan inside it! It knows exactly how to become a big plant because God designed it that way.

Common Questions About Creation

"How long was a 'day' in Genesis?" Some people think it was exactly 24 hours. Others think it might have been a long period of time. The most important thing is that God did it! He is the one who designed the system and made it work.

"What about dinosaurs?" The Bible says God made all the land animals on Day 6. That would include the big ones like the T-Rex and the tiny ones like lizards! God made every creature, even the ones that aren't around anymore.

Talk to God

Dear God, thank You for this incredible world. Thank You for the bright sun, the green grass, and the funny animals You made. When I look at creation, help me to remember how powerful and creative You are. Help me to be a good steward of the earth You gave us. Amen.

CHAPTER 5

KNOW YOU ARE MADE IN GOD'S IMAGE

In the last chapter, we saw how God made the sun, the stars, and the blue whales. Those things are all massive and beautiful. But did you know that God saved His best work for last? On the very same day He made the lions and the elephants, He made something even better. He made people.

You might think a galaxy is more impressive than a person because it is so big. Or you might think a cheetah is cooler because it can run so fast. But in God's eyes, you are the most precious thing in the entire universe. You are not just another animal. You are a special creation made to look like the King.

**"So God created mankind in his own image, in the image of
God he created them; male and female he created them."
(Genesis 1:27)**

This verse uses a very special phrase: **"the image of God."** In Latin, this is called the *Imago Dei*. It means that God built a little bit of His own character into every single human being. You are like a mirror that is meant to reflect the light of God to the rest of the world.

What Does "In His Image" Mean?

Does God have two arms, two legs, and a nose like you? Not exactly. The Bible tells us that God is Spirit. Being made in His image does not mean we look like Him on the outside. It means we are like Him on the inside.

God gave us traits that animals do not have. These traits allow us to talk to God and act like Him. Let's look at four ways you carry the image of God right now.

1. You Are Creative

God is the Great Creator. He made the world out of nothing. Because you are made in His image, you love to create things too! Think about the last time you drew a picture, built a fort, or wrote a story. You were using your imagination. Birds build nests and beavers build dams, but they always do it the same way. Only humans make art, music, and movies. When you create, you are reflecting the God who made the stars.

2. You Know Right from Wrong

Have you ever felt a "tugging" in your heart when you did something mean? That is your conscience. God is perfectly holy and just. He put a sense of "rightness" inside of you. A lion does not feel guilty after it hunts. It is just being a lion. But you know that being kind is better than being mean. You know that telling the truth is better than lying. This moral compass is a gift from God.

3. You Can Use Language

God spoke the world into existence. He is a God who communicates. He gave you the ability to use words to express your feelings and ideas. You can pray to God. You can tell your parents you love them. You can read a book and learn about the past. No other creature can use language to share complex thoughts the way humans do.

4. You Can Have Relationships

In Chapter 3, we learned that God is a Trinity. The Father, Son, and Holy Spirit have always loved each other. Since you are made in God's image, you were made for friendship too. You feel a need to belong to a family and have friends. We are happiest when we are loving others and being loved by them. This is because God is love, and He made us to be like Him.

The Big Difference: Humans vs. Animals

Sometimes people say that humans are just "smart animals." But the Bible says something different. While we should be kind to animals, they are not made in God's image.

Imagine a beautiful statue of a famous King. The statue is not the King, but it represents him. If someone spray-paints the statue, they are insulting the King. People are God's "statues" on earth. We represent Him. This is why every single person deserves respect. It doesn't matter how old they are, what they look like, or where they come from. Every person carries the thumbprint of God on their soul.

Activity 1: The Mirror Reflection Challenge

Go stand in front of a mirror. Look closely at your reflection. Now, answer these questions on a piece of paper or in your head.

1. **List three physical things about yourself:** (Example: I have brown eyes, I am tall, I have curly hair).

----

2. **List three "image" traits about yourself:** (Example: I am good at math, I like to help people, I love to sing).

----

3. **Think of a way you used your words today to help someone.**

----

4. **Think of something you created this week.**

The Lesson: The things in List 1 are your physical body. The things in List 2 and 3 are your *Imago Dei*. They are the parts of you that are like God! When you look in the mirror, don't just see your hair or your skin. See a person who was made to reflect the King of the Universe.

You Are Not an Accident

Some people think the world happened by chance. They think humans are just a lucky mistake. But the Bible says that God knit you together in your mother's womb (Psalm 139:13).

God chose your eye color. He chose your personality. He knew exactly what day you would be born. You are not a mistake. You are a masterpiece. Even if you feel like you aren't good at sports or school, you are still valuable. Your value does not come from what you *do*. Your value comes from *whose* you are. You belong to God.

God is like a Master Designer. He put "secret codes" of His own character inside of you. Use the **Secret Key** below to solve the four "Image Traits" that God gave you.

The Secret Key: 1=A, 2=E, 3=I, 4=O, 5=U
(Every number is a vowel!)

1. **CR** __ __ **T** __ **V** __ (Code: 2 − 1 − 3 − 2) *This means you can make art, music, and new things!*

2. **L** __ **V** __ **NG** (Code: 4 − 3) *This means you can care for people with all your heart.*

3. **SP** __ __ **K** __ **R** (Code: 2 − 1 − 2) *This means you use words to share big ideas and truth.*

4. **J** __ **ST** (Code: 5) *This means you want things to be fair and right.*

God didn't use a cookie cutter when He made people. He made everyone different! In the space below, create a "Profile Card" for yourself to celebrate how God made you.

- **My Name:**

  ____

- **One thing I am really good at:**

  ____

  ____

- **My favorite way to be creative:**

  ____

  ____

  ____

- **A person I can show God's love to this week:**

  ____

  ____

  ____

  ____

The Big Takeaway: You don't have to be "perfect" to reflect God. A cracked mirror can still reflect the sun! Even though we make mistakes, we still have great value because of who made us.

Home Lab: The Unique Fingerprint Art

God made you so unique that even your fingerprints are different from everyone else who has ever lived. There are billions of people on earth, but no one has your exact prints!

What you need:

- An ink pad (or a washable marker)
- White paper
- A magnifying glass (if you have one)

What to do:

1. Press your thumb onto the ink pad or color it with a washable marker.
2. Press your thumb firmly onto the white paper.
3. Do this for all ten of your fingers.
4. Use a magnifying glass to look at the tiny swirls and lines.
5. Now, use your markers to turn your fingerprints into little characters! Draw hats, legs, and arms on them.

The Lesson: Every one of those tiny lines was designed by God. He is a God of detail. If He cares enough to make your fingerprints unique, imagine how much He cares about your thoughts, your dreams, and your heart!

How Should We Treat Others?

If every person is made in God's image, how should we treat the people we meet?

- **The kid at school who is lonely:** Since they are made in God's image, they are royalty! We should show them kindness.
- **The person who is different from us:** Different skin colors or languages are just different ways God shows His creativity. We should celebrate the variety.

- **The person who is mean to us:** Even they carry God's image, though it might be "dusty" or broken by sin. We should still treat them with the respect that God's image deserves.

When we are mean to others, we are actually being disrespectful to the God who made them. When we love others, we are showing love to God.

Body and Soul

There is one more thing that makes humans special. We are made of two parts. We have a **Body** (the part you can see) and a **Soul** (the part you can't see).

Your body is like a house, and your soul is the person living inside. Your soul is the part of you that thinks, feels, and will live forever. When God made the first man, Adam, He breathed life into him. That breath made him a "living soul." Animals have the breath of life, but only humans have a soul that can know God. This is why we can pray and feel God's presence.

Talk to God

Dear God, thank You for making me in Your image. Thank You for giving me a mind to think, a heart to love, and a voice to praise You. Help me to remember how valuable I am to You. Help me to see Your image in every person I meet today. Teach me to treat others with the respect and kindness they deserve. Amen.

CHAPTER 6

FACE THE PROBLEM OF SIN

Have you ever tried to fix something that was broken? Maybe you dropped a favorite ceramic mug and it shattered into a dozen pieces. Even if you use the best glue in the world, you can still see the tiny cracks. The mug is still a mug, but it isn't "perfect" anymore.

In the last chapter, we learned that people are made in the image of God. We are like that beautiful mug. But something happened that caused a giant crack in that image. That "something" is what the Bible calls sin. To understand the rest of the Bible story, we have to look at how things got broken and why we cannot fix them on our own.

"For all have sinned and fall short of the glory of God."
(Romans 3:23)

This verse is very direct. It does not say "some" people or "bad" people have sinned. It says **all**. Imagine a high jump competition where the bar is set as high as the clouds. No matter how fast you run or how high you jump, you will always fall short of reaching it. That is what sin does. It keeps us from reaching God's perfect standard.

What Exactly is Sin?

Sin is a word we use a lot in church, but what does it mean? In the original language of the Bible, one of the words for sin comes from archery. It means **"to miss the mark."** Imagine an archer aiming for a bullseye. If the arrow hits the dirt or flies over the target, the archer missed the mark. God's "bullseye" is perfect holiness. When we do things our way instead of God's way, we miss the mark.

Sin shows up in three main ways:

1. **Doing what is wrong:** Like telling a lie or taking something that isn't yours.
2. **Not doing what is right:** Like seeing someone get bullied and staying silent instead of helping.
3. **The "I" Problem:** This is the root of sin. It is wanting to be our own boss instead of letting God be the King.

The Story of the First Crack

How did this start? It goes back to the very first two people, Adam and Eve. God put them in a perfect garden. They had everything they needed. God gave them only one rule: do not eat from the Tree of the Knowledge of Good and Evil. He gave them this rule because He loved them and wanted to protect them.

But a serpent came and whispered lies. He told them that God was holding out on them. He suggested that if they ate the fruit, they could be like God. Adam and Eve chose to believe the lie. They ate the fruit.

That one act of disobedience changed everything. It was like a drop of black ink falling into a glass of pure water. The ink spread to every part of the water. Because Adam and Eve were the heads of the human family, that "ink" of sin spread to every person born after them.

The Results of the Fall

When Adam and Eve sinned, the world "fell" away from its perfect state. This is why we call it **The Fall**. It brought three big "breaks" into the world:

- **The Break with God:** Before sin, Adam and Eve walked with God in the garden. After sin, they were afraid and tried to hide. Sin creates a giant canyon between us and God. Because God is holy, He cannot be near sin.

- **The Break with Each Other:** Have you noticed how easy it is to argue with your siblings? After the Fall, Adam blamed Eve, and Eve blamed the serpent. Sin makes us selfish, which hurts our relationships.

- **The Break with Creation:** This is why we have weeds in gardens, natural disasters, and sickness. The world is "groaning" because sin messed up the balance of nature.

Activity 1: The "Broken Image" Puzzle

Find an old cereal box or a piece of cardboard. On the plain side, draw a picture of a person (you!). Decorate it with bright colors.

1. Now, use scissors to cut the picture into 10 messy, jagged pieces.
2. Mix them up on the floor.
3. Try to put the puzzle back together.

The Lesson: You can put the pieces back in the right spot, but the lines where the paper was cut are still there. You can't make the paper "one piece" again just by pushing them together. This is like us. We are still God's masterpieces, but we are "broken" by sin. We need a Master Maker to make us new.

Imagine you are standing on one side of a deep, rocky canyon. On your side, it is dark and lonely. On the other side, it is bright, beautiful, and God is there. You want to get to the other side, but there is no bridge.

In the Bible, our "good works" are like trying to build a bridge. We might try to use wood (being kind) or stones (going to church) or rope (obeying rules). But no matter how hard we try, our bridge is always too short to reach the other side.

Fill in the blanks below to see why we can't cross the gap on our own:

1. **THE GAP:** The name of the big canyon that keeps us away from God is called

    S __ __. (Hint: It rhymes with "pin").

2. **THE JUMP:** If the canyon is 100 feet wide and you jump 10 feet, do you make it? (Yes or No).

3. **THE TRUTH:** Even if you are the "best" kid in the world, can you be as perfect as God? (Yes or No).

The Lesson: We cannot build a bridge to God by being "good enough." We need someone from the other side to come and rescue us.

Is There Any Good News?

Reading about sin can feel a bit sad. It's a big problem! But we have to understand the bad news so we can truly love the Good News.

If you didn't know you were sick, you wouldn't go to the doctor. If you didn't know the house was on fire, you wouldn't call for help. Understanding sin helps us realize that we need a Savior.

The Bible says that while we were still sinners, God already had a plan to fix the "cracks." He didn't leave us in the dark forest. He didn't leave us on the other side of the canyon. He decided to build a bridge. We will learn all about that bridge in the next few chapters!

Sin starts small, but it gets very heavy.

What you need:

- A backpack
- Several heavy books or rocks

What to do:

1. Put on the empty backpack. Walk around the room. It feels light and easy, right?

2. Now, have someone add one heavy book. This represents a "small" sin, like a tiny lie. Walk again.

3. Add five more books. These represent more sins—disobeying parents, being mean, putting yourself first.

4. Try to run or jump with the full backpack.

The Lesson: Sin is a burden. It slows us down and makes us tired. It keeps us from being the joyful, free people God made us to be. Only Jesus can take that backpack off our shoulders and give us rest.

Activity 3: Clear the Vowels

God wants to wash us clean. Below are some words about sin, but the vowels (A, E, I, O, U) have been replaced by a "scrum" of ink. Can you figure out the words?

1. G __ __ L T (The feeling we have when we do wrong)
2. H __ D __ NG (What Adam and Eve did in the garden)
3. PR __ D __ (Thinking we are better than others)
4. L __ __ S (Words that are not true)

Answers: 1. GUILT, 2. HIDING, 3. PRIDE, 4. LIES

Talk to God

Dear God, I know that I have missed the mark. I have done things my own way instead of Your way. Thank You for showing me the truth about sin so that I can see how much I need You. Thank You that You don't leave me alone in my mistakes. Help me to be honest about my sin and look to You for help. Amen.

CHAPTER 7

MEET JESUS, THE PROMISED SAVIOR

If you have ever played a game of hide-and-seek, you know the feeling of being "found." In the last chapter, we saw how sin made Adam and Eve want to hide from God. But God didn't want them to stay hidden. He didn't want the "crack" in the world to stay broken forever.

Immediately after the Fall, God made a promise. He promised that one day, a Savior would come to crush the power of sin and death. Thousands of years went by, and God kept dropping clues through the prophets about who this Savior would be. Finally, in a small stable in Bethlehem, the Promise arrived.

"She will give birth to a son, and you are to give him the name Jesus, because he will save his people from their sins." (Matthew 1:21)

The name **Jesus** actually means "The Lord Saves." It wasn't just a popular name back then; it was His job description! Jesus didn't come to earth just to be a good teacher or a famous leader. He came for a specific mission: to be the bridge across the gap of sin.

Who is Jesus? (The Two Truths)

To understand Jesus, you have to hold two big ideas in your head at the same time. This is called the **Hypostatic Union** (that's a giant phrase to impress your parents with!). It simply means:

1. **Jesus is 100% God:** He is the Son of God. He has always existed. He has all the power and holiness of God because He *is* God.

2. **Jesus is 100% Man:** He was born as a baby. He grew up, He got hungry, He got tired, and He felt pain. He had a human heart and a human brain.

Why does this matter? Because to bridge the gap between God and humans, the Savior had to belong to both sides! He had to be a man so He could represent us, and He had to be God so He could be perfect enough to pay for our sins.

The Perfect Life

Think back to the "Archery" example from Chapter 6. Everyone else who has ever lived has "missed the mark." We have all sinned. But Jesus lived for about 33 years and **never once missed.**

- He never told a lie to get out of trouble.
- He never had a selfish thought.
- He always obeyed His parents and His Heavenly Father.
- He always loved people perfectly, even the ones who were mean to Him.

Because Jesus was perfect, He was the only person in history who didn't deserve to be punished for sin. This is what made Him the perfect "Substitute."

The Three Offices of Jesus

In the Old Testament, God used three types of people to lead His people. Jesus came to be the "Ultimate" version of all three:

- **The Prophet:** A prophet brings God's Word to the people. Jesus didn't just *bring* the Word; He *is* the Word. He taught us exactly how God wants us to live.

- **The Priest:** A priest stands between God and people to offer sacrifices. Jesus didn't just *offer* a sacrifice; He *was* the sacrifice. He is our way to talk to God.

- **The King:** A king rules over his kingdom. Jesus is the King of kings. He rules with love and kindness, and His kingdom will never end.

Activity 1: The "Who is Jesus?" Fill-in-the-Blank

Use the words in the **Word Bank** to complete the sentences about Jesus.

Word Bank: *Bridge, Perfect, Savior, God, Man*

1. Jesus is fully __________ and fully __________.
2. Because Jesus never sinned, His life was __________.
3. Jesus is the __________ that connects us back to God.
4. The name "Jesus" means the Lord is our __________.

Activity 2: The Prophet, Priest, and King Roles

Jesus has three main "jobs" or titles. Fill in the missing letters to name them!

1. **PR__PH__T:** He teaches us God's Word and tells us the truth.
2. **PR__ __ST:** He stands between us and God to help us be friends with Him.
3. **K__NG:** He is the boss of the whole universe and rules with love.

The Greatest Rescue Mission

Imagine you are trapped in a deep, dark pit. You try to climb out, but the walls are too slippery. A teacher walks by and shouts, "You should have been more careful!" A philosopher walks by and says, "Just imagine you aren't in a pit."

But then, Jesus comes by. He doesn't just give you advice from the top. He climbs down into the pit with you, puts you on His shoulders, and carries you out.

That is what the "Incarnation" (God becoming human) is all about. Jesus left the perfect beauty of heaven to come into our messy, sinful world. He did it because He loves you and didn't want to be in heaven without you.

Home Lab: The "Weight Lifter" Demonstration

Remember the backpack full of books from Chapter 6? Let's see what Jesus does with that weight.

What you need:

- The heavy backpack (from the Chapter 6 Home Lab)
- A strong volunteer (like a parent or older sibling)

What to do:

1. Put on the heavy backpack. Try to do five jumping jacks. It's hard!

2. Now, have your volunteer stand behind you and lift the bottom of the backpack while you jump.

3. Finally, take the backpack off and give it to the volunteer. Let them wear it while you run around.

The Lesson: Jesus saw that the weight of our sin was too heavy for us to carry. He didn't just help us lift it; He took it from us completely. He carried the weight of the whole world's sin so that we could be free and "light."

Below, write the name **JESUS** in big, bold letters. Decorate it with things that represent His roles:

- Draw a small **Crown** over the "J" (for King).
- Draw a small **Cross** in the "S" (for Savior).
- Draw a small **Scroll** or Book under the "U" (for Teacher/Prophet).

Jesus being born and living a perfect life was the first half of the rescue. But there was a debt that had to be paid. In the next chapter, we are going to look at the most important Friday in history, the day Jesus gave everything to bring us home.

Talk to God

Dear Jesus, thank You for coming to earth for me. Thank You for being the perfect Bridge between me and God. I am amazed that You are the King of the universe, yet You care about my life. Help me to learn from Your teachings and follow You as my King. Amen.

CHAPTER 8

ACCEPT THE GIFT OF GRACE

Imagine it is your birthday. You wake up early, race to the living room, and see a box sitting on the table. It is wrapped in the shiny, golden paper you love, topped with a massive, curly red bow. Your name is written on the tag in big, bold letters.

You didn't build this gift. You didn't work a job to pay for it. You didn't even have to clean your room perfectly to "deserve" it. Your parents bought it because they love you. To make it yours, you only have to do one thing: reach out, pull the ribbon, and open the box.

In the last chapter, we saw the incredible price Jesus paid on the Cross. He did the hard work. He paid the "bill" for our sin. Now, He stands before you with a gift in His hands. That gift is called **Grace**. In this chapter, we are going to explore exactly what Grace is, why it is so different from everything else in the world, and how you can officially open it.

"For the wages of sin is death, but the gift of God is eternal life in Christ Jesus our Lord." (Romans 6:23)

This verse explains the "Great Exchange" perfectly. A **wage** is something you earn. If you do chores for an hour and get five dollars, that is your wage. Because of our sin, the "wage" we earned was to be separated from God. But the second half of the verse is the Good News! It says that life with God isn't a wage we earn, it is a **free gift**. Gifts aren't earned; they are simply received with a thankful heart.

What Exactly is Grace?

The word "Grace" is one of the most important words in the entire Bible. To understand it, we have to compare it to two other words: **Justice** and **Mercy**.

1. Justice (Getting what you deserve)

Imagine you accidentally broke a neighbor's window while playing ball. Justice means you have to pay to fix the window. You did the damage, so you pay the price. In our life with God, Justice would mean we stay separated from Him because of our sin.

2. Mercy (NOT getting what you deserve)

Imagine your neighbor sees the broken window, looks at you, and says, "I know you're sorry. I'm not going to make you pay for it. I forgive you." That is Mercy. It's when the punishment we earned is taken away.

3. Grace (Getting what you DON'T deserve)

Now, imagine the neighbor not only forgives you for the window but also invites you inside, gives you a giant slice of chocolate cake, and hands you a brand-new, better baseball. That is **Grace**! It is God giving us His love, His friendship, and a home in Heaven, even though we didn't do anything to earn it.

The Story of the Two Builders

Let's imagine two people trying to reach a beautiful island in the middle of a vast sea.

Builder A thinks he can get there by working hard. He starts swimming as fast as he can. He swims for hours, but the island is hundreds of miles away. No matter how hard he tries, he gets tired and realizes he will never be strong enough to make it on his own. He is trying to reach God through "works."

Builder B knows he can't swim that far. He stands on the shore and waits. Suddenly, a massive, beautiful ship pulls up. The Captain leans over the side and says, "I have already sailed to the island and back. I have plenty of room. Do you want to come with me for free?"

Following Jesus is like getting on the ship. The "Ship of Grace" carries us where we could never go on our own.

Activity 1: Reflections on Grace

In the space below, answer these three questions in your own words.

1. Think of a time you were given a gift you didn't expect. How did it feel to receive it without having to "work" for it?

    ----

2. Why do you think God chose to make salvation a **gift** instead of something we have to earn?

    ----

3. Based on what we learned about "Justice" and "Grace," what is the biggest difference between the two?

Even though a gift is free, it doesn't do you any good if it just sits on the table. If your friend offers you a piece of candy, it doesn't become yours until you reach out your hand and take it.

In the Bible, **Faith** is the "hand" that reaches out to take the gift of Grace. Faith isn't just a feeling; it is **trust**.

The ABCs of Faith

We often use these three letters to help us remember how to reach out and take God's gift:

- **A – Admit:** You admit that you have sinned. You tell God, "I know I can't reach the 'island' by swimming on my own. I need Your help."

- **B – Believe:** You believe that Jesus is the Son of God and that His death on the cross paid for your sins. You trust that the "Ship" is strong enough to carry you.

- **C – Choose:** You choose to let Jesus be the King of your life. You decide to step onto the ship and go where He leads.

The Great Swap

When you accept the gift of Grace, something amazing happens that the Bible calls "Justification." It sounds like a big legal word, but it just means "Just-as-if-I'd" never sinned.

Imagine you are wearing a white t-shirt that is covered in mud, grass stains, and ink. That represents our sin. Now imagine Jesus is wearing a robe that is perfectly white, glowing, and clean.

Grace is when Jesus walks up to you and says, "Let's trade." He takes your stained shirt and puts it on Himself. Then, He takes His perfect, clean robe and puts it on you. Now, when God looks at you, He doesn't see the "mud" of your mistakes. He sees the "white robe" of Jesus!

Faith really just means **Trust**. Think about these everyday examples of faith:

- When you sit in a chair, you have "faith" that it won't break.
- When you turn on a faucet, you have "faith" that water will come out.

In the space below, write down three other things you "trust" every single day:

1. ____
2. ____
3. ____

The Big Point: Salvation is putting that same kind of trust in Jesus. You are "sitting down" on His promise that He has saved you.

Home Lab: The "Penny and the Vinegar" Clean-Up

This experiment shows that we can't make ourselves clean, but a "solution" from the outside can!

What you need:

- A few very old, dirty, brown pennies.
- A small bowl of vinegar mixed with a spoonful of salt.
- A paper towel.

What to do:

1. Look at the pennies. They are covered in "oxidation" (the dark brown stuff). You can't rub it off with your fingers.
2. Drop the pennies into the vinegar and salt. Count to 20.
3. Take them out and rinse them with water.

The Lesson: The pennies didn't "work hard" to get shiny. They just had to be "submerged" in the solution. When we "immerse" ourselves in God's grace, He washes away the old, dirty parts of our character and makes us shine like new!

"Do I have to be 'extra good' after I get the gift?" You don't do good things to *get* the gift, but you will *want* to do good things because you are so thankful for the gift! Imagine someone saved your life—you would want to be their best friend and help them however you could, right? That is why we follow God's rules—out of love, not out of fear.

"What if I make a mistake tomorrow?" Grace doesn't run out. If you mess up, you don't lose the gift. You just go back to God, tell Him you're sorry, and He helps you get back on track. His Grace is new every single morning.

Talk to God

If you want to accept this gift today, or if you just want to thank God for it, you can talk to Him right now:

"Dear God, thank You for the Gift of Grace. I admit that I have sinned and I can't fix it on my own. I believe that Jesus died for me and rose again to pay my debt. Today, I choose to take Your hand and follow You. Thank You for loving me even when I make mistakes. Help me to live a life that shows how thankful I am for Your gift. Amen."

CHAPTER 9

WALK WITH THE HOLY SPIRIT

Have you ever tried to find your way through a thick forest at night? Or maybe you've tried to put together a 1,000-piece puzzle without the picture on the box? It is hard to do things alone when you don't have a guide or a helper.

In the last chapter, we learned about the amazing gift of Grace. When you accept that gift, God doesn't just give you a "ticket to heaven" and then leave you to figure the rest of your life out by yourself. He gives you a Helper. That Helper is the **Holy Spirit**. In this chapter, we are going to learn who the Holy Spirit is and how He helps us walk through life every single day.

**"But the Advocate, the Holy Spirit, whom the Father will
send in my name, will teach you all things and will remind
you of everything I have said to you." (John 14:26)**

Before Jesus went back to heaven, He promised His friends that He wouldn't leave them as orphans. He promised to send the Holy Spirit. Think about that: the same God who created the stars and the same Jesus who walked on water now lives **inside** of you through the Holy Spirit. You never have to go anywhere alone again!

Who is the Holy Spirit?

Sometimes people get confused about the Holy Spirit. He isn't a "ghost" like you see in movies, and He isn't just a "feeling." The Holy Spirit is **God**. Remember back in Chapter 3 when we talked about the Trinity? The Holy Spirit is the third Person of the Trinity.

Because He is God, He is powerful, wise, and kind. When you become a Christian, the Holy Spirit comes to live in your heart. This is called "Indwelling." He becomes your constant companion.

The Three Jobs of the Holy Spirit

The Holy Spirit is very busy! He has several special jobs He does in your life:

1. The Comforter

In the Bible, one of the names for the Holy Spirit is "Paraclete," which means "one who walks alongside." When you are sad, lonely, or scared, the Holy Spirit provides a peace that doesn't make sense to the rest of the world. He reminds you that God loves you and that you are safe.

2. The Teacher

Have you ever read a Bible verse and thought, *"I have no idea what this means"*? That is when you can ask the Holy Spirit for help! He is the one who wrote the Bible (through human authors), so He is the best teacher in the world. He helps the "lights go on" in your brain so you can understand God's truth.

3. The Compass

A compass tells a traveler which way is North so they don't get lost. The Holy Spirit acts like a spiritual compass. He "convicts" us, which is a church word for a "nudge" in our heart, when we are about to do something wrong. He also guides us toward the right choices, like being kind to a new student or telling the truth even when it's hard.

Activity 1: The Helper's Roles

Based on what you just read, think about your own life. Write down a time when you might need the Holy Spirit to do one of these jobs for you.

- **I need the Comforter when:**

- **I need the Teacher when:**

- **I need the Compass when:**

The Fruit of the Spirit

How can you tell if the Holy Spirit is really working in someone? You look at their "fruit." Just like an apple tree produces apples, a person who "walks with the Spirit" produces certain qualities.

The Bible says the **Fruit of the Spirit** is Love, Joy, Peace, Patience, Kindness, Goodness, Faithfulness, Gentleness, and Self-Control (Galatians 5:22-23).

Notice that the Bible says "fruit" (singular), not "fruits" (plural). It's like a bunch of grapes; they all grow together! You can't grow these by trying really hard to be "good." Instead, as you spend time with the

Holy Spirit, He grows them in you. You might notice that you are suddenly more patient with your siblings or more joyful even when things go wrong. That's the Holy Spirit at work!

Activity 2: Fruit Check-In

Look at the nine Fruits of the Spirit listed above.

1. Which fruit do you see growing in your life right now? Give an example.

____

____

____

____

____

2. Which fruit do you want the Holy Spirit to help you grow more of?

____

____

____

____

____

How Do We "Walk" with the Spirit?

"Walking with the Spirit" just means staying in step with Him. Imagine you are walking with a friend. If you run way ahead, you can't hear them. If you stop and sit down, they leave you behind. To walk with them, you have to stay close and listen.

We stay close to the Spirit by:

- **Listening:** When you feel that "nudge" in your heart to do something good, do it!

- **Asking:** Start your day by saying, "Holy Spirit, help me to follow You today."

- **Filling Up:** Spend time in the Bible so the Spirit has God's Word to use to guide you.

The Bible often compares the Holy Spirit to the wind. You can't see the wind, but you can see what it **does**.

What you need:

- A small paper boat (or a toy boat).
- A tub of water.
- Your own breath (or a small fan).

What to do:

1. Put the boat in the water. It just sits there, right? It has no power to move on its own.
2. Now, blow gently on the sail. Watch the boat move across the water.
3. Try blowing from different directions.

The Lesson: We are like the boat. On our own, we don't have the power to live a "God-sized" life. But the Holy Spirit is like the wind. When we "set our sails" toward Him, He provides the power to move us in the right direction. He does the work; we just have to catch the wind!

Talk to God

"Dear Holy Spirit, thank You for being my Helper. Thank You for living in my heart and promising never to leave me. Please be my Teacher when I read the Bible and my Compass when I have to make hard choices. Grow Your fruit in my life so that others can see Jesus in me. Amen."

CHAPTER 10

JOIN THE FAMILY OF GOD

Imagine for a moment that you are standing outside a grand, beautiful house during a rainstorm. Inside, you can see a large family sitting around a fireplace. They are laughing, sharing a meal, and telling stories. There is a sense of warmth and safety in that room that you can feel even through the window. You want to go inside, but you aren't sure if you belong. Then, the front door swings wide open, and the Father of the house stands there with a smile. He doesn't ask for your ID card, and he doesn't ask if you've worked hard enough to earn a seat at the table. He simply says, "Welcome home. You're part of the family now."

In our previous chapters, we learned about the incredible **Grace** of God and how the **Holy Spirit** comes to live within us as our Helper. But being a Christian isn't just a "me and God" thing. When you accept the gift of salvation, you aren't just rescued; you are **adopted**. You have been brought into a massive, worldwide, eternal family. In this chapter, we are going to explore what it means to be a child of God, how we treat our new brothers and sisters, and the amazing organization God created to keep us together: **The Church.**

"See what great love the Father has lavished on us, that we should be called children of God! And that is what we are! The reason the world does not know us is that it did not know him." (1 John 3:1)

Notice that the Bible doesn't say God "gave" us a little bit of love. It says He **lavished** it on us. To lavish something means to pour it out in huge, overflowing amounts, like pouring a whole gallon of chocolate syrup on one scoop of ice cream! God didn't just forgive your sins; He went much further. He changed your status. You went from being a stranger to being a son or a daughter of the King of the Universe.

In the world we live in, adoption happens when a family chooses a child to be their very own. They sign legal papers that say, "This child is now ours. They have our name. They have a right to everything we own. They are just as much a part of this family as if they were born into it."

The Bible says that is exactly what God did for you.

- **He Chose You:** God didn't wait for you to find Him; He sought you out.
- **He Gave You His Name:** We are called "Christians" because we carry the name of Christ.
- **He Shares His Inheritance:** Everything that belongs to Jesus, peace, joy, and eternal life, now belongs to you, too.

Because God is your Father, every other person who trusts in Jesus is your brother or sister. This family is bigger than any sports team fan base or any country. It includes people who speak languages you've never heard, people who eat foods you've never tasted, and people who lived hundreds of years before you were even born!

When you meet another Christian, even if they live on the other side of the planet, you have something in common that is stronger than anything else: you share the same Father.

Activity 1: My Family Traits

When people are in the same family, they often look alike. Spiritual family members have "traits" too! Based on what we've learned, what are three things that should show up in the lives of God's children?

1. ____

2. ____

3. ____

What is "The Church"?

When many people hear the word "church," they think of a building with a steeple, some stained glass, and wooden benches. While those buildings are nice, they aren't actually the Church.

The Church is the People. The word used in the Bible for church is *ekklesia*, which means "a gathered assembly." It's like a giant team huddle. The building is just the locker room where the team meets to get instructions from the Coach (God) before going out to play the game (living for God in the world).

The Body of Christ

The Bible uses a very cool metaphor to explain how the Church works. It says the Church is like a **human body**.

- **Jesus is the Head:** He is the brain that tells the body what to do.

- **We are the Parts:** Some of us are hands, some are feet, some are ears, and some are eyes.

Think about how your own body works. Your hand is great at picking things up, but it can't hear a song. Your ear is great at hearing music, but it can't walk to the kitchen. For the body to work, every part has to do its job, and every part has to stay connected to the head.

If you decide you don't need the Church, it's like a finger trying to live all by itself on a table. It won't work! We need each other to be healthy.

64

Every person in God's family has been given a "gift" or a "talent" to help the rest of the family. Look at the list below and circle the ones you think you might be good at:

- **Encouraging:** Saying kind words to someone who is sad.
- **Serving:** Helping clean up or setting up for an event.
- **Giving:** Sharing your things or money with people in need.
- **Teaching:** Explaining Bible stories to younger kids.
- **Leading:** Helping organize a group to get a task done.
- **Listening:** Being a good friend to someone who needs to talk.

How can you use one of these "parts" this week to help your church family?

The "One Anothers"

Because we are family, God gave us specific instructions on how to treat each other. In the New Testament, there are over 50 "one another" commands. Here are a few of the most important ones:

1. **Love one another:** This is the big one! Jesus said people would know we follow Him by how much we love our church family.

2. **Forgive one another:** Families have disagreements. Sometimes brothers and sisters are mean or selfish. But because God forgave us, we have to be quick to forgive each other.

3. **Carry one another's burdens:** If a family member is going through a hard time, maybe they are sick or sad, the rest of the family steps in to help carry the weight.

4. **Pray for one another:** We talk to our Father about the needs of our brothers and sisters.

Sometimes, on a rainy Sunday morning, it might feel easier to stay in bed and watch cartoons. But gathering with the family of God is like charging a battery. When you go to church, three important things happen:

- **Instruction:** You learn more about God's Word so you can grow strong.

- **Worship:** You join your voice with others to tell God how great He is. There is something powerful about singing with hundreds of other people!

- **Fellowship:** You spend time with friends who believe what you believe. They remind you that you aren't alone in following Jesus.

Home Lab: The "Coal and the Fire" Demonstration

This shows why staying connected to the Church family is so important for your faith.

What you need:

- A parent or adult to help you (this involves a grill or a fireplace).

- A pile of charcoal or wood.

What to do:

1. Look at a pile of burning coals in a grill. When they are all bunched together, they stay red-hot and create a lot of heat.

2. Have an adult use tongs to take one single coal out of the pile and move it to the far corner of the grill, all by itself.

3. Watch what happens to that one coal over the next few minutes.

The Lesson: The coal that was moved away from the others will quickly turn grey and lose its heat. It didn't "stop being coal," but it lost its fire. We are just like those coals. When we stay close to other Christians, our "fire" for God stays hot. If we try to do it all alone, our faith can get cold and grey. We need the "heat" of our church family!

In the space below, draw a picture of your "Church Family." It doesn't have to be everyone in the building! Draw your Sunday school teacher, your pastor, or the friends you play with at church.

Write one reason you are thankful for the people in your drawing:

What If the Church Isn't Perfect?

Have you ever had a fight with your brother or sister? Of course! Even though we are God's family, we are still people who make mistakes. Sometimes people in the church are mean, or they say things that hurt our feelings.

When that happens, remember this: the Church is not a museum for perfect people; it is a **hospital** for people who are healing. We are all "under construction." Just because a family member makes a mistake doesn't mean they aren't your family anymore. We stay, we forgive, and we help each other grow.

Talk to God

"Dear Father, thank You for adopting me into Your family. It is amazing to know that I am Your child and that I have brothers and sisters all over the world. Thank You for my church and for the people who help me learn about You. Help me to be a good 'part of the body' and to use my gifts to help others. Teach me how to love and forgive my church family just like You love and forgive me. Amen."

CHAPTER 11

TALK WITH YOUR HEAVENLY FATHER

Imagine for a moment that you found a secret, golden telephone hidden in a drawer in your room. This isn't a normal phone; it doesn't need a charger, it never loses its signal, and it only has one number saved in it. If you pick up that phone, the person on the other end is the King of the Universe. He isn't too busy to talk. He doesn't put you on hold. He doesn't have an assistant tell you to "call back later." The moment you whisper a word, He is listening with 100% of His attention.

In the last chapter, we learned that you are now a part of God's family. One of the greatest privileges of being a child of God is that you have a direct line to your Father. We call this **Prayer**.

Many people think prayer is a scary, formal thing that you only do in church while wearing fancy clothes and using old-fashioned words. But the truth is much more exciting. Prayer is simply **talking to God**. It is a conversation between a child and a Father who loves them more than anything. In this chapter, we are going to learn how to talk to God, what to say, and how to listen for His voice.

The Focus Verse

"Do not be anxious about anything, but in every situation, by prayer and petition, with thanksgiving, present your requests to God." (Philippians 4:6)

Notice the words **"in everything."** God doesn't just want to hear about the "big" stuff, like when someone is sick or when you have a big test. He wants to hear about the small stuff, too! He wants to know about the cool bug you found, the joke that made you laugh, and the thing that made you feel a little bit lonely at lunch. If it matters to you, it matters to Him.

How Do We Pray?

Some kids worry that they don't know the "right" words to say. They think if they don't say "Amen" at the right time or use big words, God won't hear them. But remember, God is your Father. Does a dad care if his toddler uses perfect grammar when they say, "I love you"? Of course not! He just loves hearing their voice.

You can pray:

- **Out loud or in your head:** God hears your thoughts just as clearly as your words.

- **With your eyes open or closed:** Closing your eyes just helps you focus, but you can pray while walking to school or riding your bike!

- **Anywhere and anytime:** You don't have to be in a church building. You can pray in bed, on the playground, or in the middle of a crowded room.

The P.R.A.Y. Method

If you aren't sure where to start, you can use the word **P.R.A.Y.** to help you remember four great things to talk to God about:

P – Praise (Adoration)

Start by telling God how great He is. This isn't for His benefit (He already knows He's great!), it's for ours. It helps us remember how big and powerful our Father is.

- *Example: "God, You are so creative! Thank You for making the mountains and the oceans."*

R – Repent (Confession)

This is where we are honest about our mistakes. We tell God we are sorry for the times we "missed the mark" today. Because of Grace, we don't have to be afraid to tell Him the truth.

- *Example: "Father, I'm sorry I was mean to my sister this morning. Please help me to be kind."*

A – Ask (Petition)

This is where we tell God what we need. It's okay to ask for things! We can ask for help for ourselves and for other people.

- *Example: "Please help my Grandma feel better, and help me not to be nervous about my math test."*

Y – Yield (Thanksgiving)

To yield means to say, "I trust Your plan more than mine." We thank Him for what He has already done and tell Him we trust Him with the future.

- *Example: "Thank You for my family. I trust You to lead me today. Your way is the best way."*

Activity 1: My P.R.A.Y. Journal

Use the space below to write a short prayer using the four steps we just learned.

- P (Praise): ____
- R (Repent): ____
- A (Ask): ____
- Y (Yield/Thank): ____

Does God Always Answer?

This is a big question. Sometimes we pray for something—like a sick pet to get better—and it doesn't happen the way we wanted. Does that mean God didn't hear us? No. God always answers, but He answers like a wise Father, not a vending machine.

Think of it this way. A Father can say three things:

1. **YES:** "I love that idea! Here it is."
2. **NO:** "I love you too much to give you that, because I know it will hurt you or it isn't what's best."
3. **WAIT:** "Not yet. I have something better planned, but you have to trust Me and be patient."

God sees the "whole picture" of your life. We only see one small piece of the puzzle. When God says "No" or "Wait," it's because He loves us, not because He isn't listening.

The Model Prayer: The Lord's Prayer

One day, Jesus' disciples asked Him, "Lord, teach us to pray." Jesus gave them a beautiful example that we still use today. It's called **The Lord's Prayer.**

In this prayer, Jesus shows us that we should start by honoring God's name, asking for His Kingdom to come on earth, and asking for our "daily bread" (the things we need to get through the day). He also reminds us to ask for forgiveness and to ask for protection from temptation.

Activity 2: Daily Bread Check-In

What are three things you need "daily bread" for today? It could be patience, energy, food, or a brave heart.

1. ____
2. ____
3. ____

If you went to a friend's house and talked for an hour without letting them say a single word, would that be a very good conversation? Probably not! Prayer is a two-way street. We talk to God, but we also have to **listen** to Him.

How does God "talk" back?

- **Through His Word:** Most of the time, God answers our prayers through the verses we read in the Bible.
- **Through the Holy Spirit:** As we learned in Chapter 9, the Spirit gives us "nudges" or quiet thoughts in our hearts.
- **Through Other People:** Sometimes a parent or teacher says exactly what we needed to hear.
- **Through Circumstances:** Sometimes God opens or closes a door to show us which way to go.

Home Lab: The "Cup Phone" Experiment

This experiment shows how communication works and how we need to stay "connected" to hear clearly.

What you need:

- Two paper cups.
- A long piece of string (about 10–15 feet).
- A paperclip or tape.

What to do:

1. Poke a small hole in the bottom of each cup.
2. Thread the string through the holes and tie a knot (or use a paperclip) to keep the string from pulling out.
3. Give one cup to a partner and walk away until the string is **tight**.
4. Whisper into your cup while your partner holds theirs to their ear.

The Lesson: If the string is loose or floppy, the sound won't travel. You can't hear anything! But when the string is pulled tight, the connection is clear. Prayer is our "string" to God. When we stay focused and "tight" in our relationship with Him, we can hear His heart more clearly.

One of the most powerful things you can do is pray for someone else. This is called **Intercession**.

Who can you pray for today?

- A Family Member: ____

- A Friend: ____

- A Teacher or Leader: ____

- Someone who is hurting: ____

Talk to God

"Dear Heavenly Father, thank You that I don't need a special phone or a fancy building to talk to You. Thank You for listening to me every time I pray. Help me to remember to talk to You about everything, the big things and the small things. Teach me how to listen for Your voice in my heart and in Your Word. I am so glad that You are my Father. Amen."

CHAPTER 12

LIVE A LIFE FOR GOD'S GLORY

Have you ever seen a mirror in a dark room? If there is no light, the mirror doesn't look like much. It's just a dark, cold piece of glass. But the moment you turn on a lamp or open the curtains to let the sun in, something amazing happens. The mirror begins to shine! It looks like there is a light *inside* the mirror, but we know the truth: the mirror is simply reflecting the light from somewhere else.

This is the secret to living a life for **God's Glory**. In the previous chapters, we learned how to talk to God, how to walk with the Spirit, and how to belong to His family. Now, we ask the big question: *"What am I supposed to do with my life?"*

The answer is simpler than you might think. You are called to be God's mirror. You aren't the source of the light, but you are designed to reflect His beauty, His kindness, and His love to everyone around you. Living for God's glory means making Him look as great to others as He truly is.

"So whether you eat or drink or whatever you do, do it all for the glory of God." (1 Corinthians 10:31)

Did you catch that? Even the smallest, most normal things, like eating a sandwich or drinking a glass of water, can be done for God's glory. You don't have to be a preacher on a stage or a missionary in a jungle to glorify God. You can glorify Him in your classroom, on the soccer field, while doing your chores, or while playing with your friends.

What Does "Glory" Actually Mean?

"Glory" is a big church word, but in the Bible, it often carries the idea of **weight** or **importance**. To glorify God means to show the world that He is the most important thing in your life.

Imagine you have a backpack. If you fill it with feathers, it's light and unimportant. But if you fill it with gold bricks, it becomes heavy and valuable. When we glorify God, we are telling the world, "God isn't a 'feather' in my life; He is the 'gold.' He is the most valuable person I know."

The Three Ways We Reflect God's Glory:
1. **Our Words:** How we speak to our parents, our teachers, and even people who are mean to us.
2. **Our Actions:** The choices we make when no one is watching.
3. **Our Attitude:** Having a heart of thankfulness instead of complaining.

Activity 1: The Glory Spotlight

Imagine you are a stage director and you have a giant spotlight. You can point it at yourself to make everyone look at you, or you can point it at God to make everyone look at Him.

In the situations below, how can you "turn the spotlight" toward God?

- **Situation 1:** You just won a trophy for being the best player on your team.

- o *Instead of saying "I'm the best," you could say:*

- **Situation 2:** You see a student at school sitting all alone and crying.

  - o *To show God's kindness, you could:*

- **Situation 3:** Your mom asks you to clean your room when you really want to play video games.

  - o *To glorify God with your attitude, you could:*

The "Salt and Light" Mission

Jesus gave us two very cool nicknames to help us understand our mission in the world. He called us the **Salt of the Earth** and the **Light of the World**.

1. You are the Salt

Have you ever eaten a french fry without salt? It's a bit bland, right? Salt does two things: it adds flavor and it preserves things (keeps them from rotting). As a Christian, your life should "add flavor" to the world. You should be the person who brings joy, peace, and kindness into a room. You also "preserve" the world by standing up for what is right when others are doing what is wrong.

2. You are the Light

Light does one main thing: it chases away the dark. In a world that can sometimes be dark with sadness, anger, or lies, your life should be a bright spot. You don't have to be a giant bonfire; even a tiny candle can help someone find their way in a dark room.

Think about your "world": your home, your school, and your neighborhood. Where is one "dark" spot where you could bring some light this week? (Maybe a lonely neighbor, a messy park, or a friend who is sad).

My Plan to Shine: "This week, I will ____________________________

because I want to ____

show God's glory to ______________________________________

The Heart of a Servant

One of the best ways to glorify God is by **serving**. Jesus is the King of Kings, but when He was on earth, He did something shocking. He put on a towel and washed His disciples' dirty, dusty feet. He showed us that the greatest people in God's Kingdom are the ones who help others.

Serving isn't always about big projects. It's about having "servant eyes." This means looking around and asking, *"Who needs help right now?"* * It's picking up a piece of trash that isn't yours.

- It's letting someone else go first in line.
- It's helping your teacher move chairs without being asked.

When you serve others, people often ask, "Why are you being so nice?" That is your chance to tell them, "Because God has been so good to me!"

Home Lab: The "Glow in the Dark" Discovery

This experiment shows how we need to stay close to the Light to reflect the Light.

What you need:

- Something that "glows in the dark" (like a plastic star or a glow-stick).
- A very bright lamp or a sunny window.
- A dark closet.

What to do:

1. Take your glow-in-the-dark object into the dark closet. It probably doesn't glow very much.
2. Now, hold the object right up against a bright light bulb for 60 seconds. (Be careful not to touch the hot bulb!)
3. Immediately go back into the dark closet.

The Lesson: The object glows because it "soaked up" the light from the lamp. It can't glow on its own. If you want your life to "glow" with God's glory, you have to spend time close to Him in prayer and in His Word. The closer you stay to the Light, the brighter you will shine!

Living for an Audience of One

Sometimes we try to do good things because we want people to clap for us or tell us how great we are. But if we do that, we are glorifying ourselves, not God.

Living for God's glory means living for an **"Audience of One."** This means that even if no one else sees you do the right thing, you are happy because you know God sees you.

- If you find a dollar on the floor and turn it in to the teacher, and no one ever finds out it was you, God saw it, and He is glorified.
- If you work really hard on your homework even when you're tired, God saw it, and He is glorified.

When we live for Him, we don't need the world to clap. We are waiting for the day when we hear Him say, *"Well done, good and faithful servant."*

Activity 3: The Glory Log

For the next 24 hours, try to keep a "Glory Log." Every time you do something, no matter how small, with the goal of making God look good, write it down here.

Talk to God

"Dear Heavenly Father, thank You for the privilege of being Your mirror. I want my life to show the world how wonderful, kind, and powerful You are. Help me to have 'servant eyes' so I can see who needs help today. Whether I am playing, studying, or helping at home, help me to do it all for Your glory. Let my light shine so that others will see my good works and praise You. Amen."

CHAPTER 13

LOOK FORWARD TO A NEW HOME

Have you ever been on a long car ride to a place you really love? Maybe it's a trip to a theme park, your grandparent's house, or the beach. The car ride might be bumpy, you might get tired of sitting still, and you might even ask, "Are we there yet?" a dozen times. But the whole time you are in the car, you have a smile on your face because you know where you are going. The destination makes the journey worth it.

Our life on earth is a lot like that car ride. In the last twelve chapters, we have learned how to know God, how to follow Jesus, and how to live for His glory right now. But the story of the Bible doesn't end on earth. God has promised us a final destination that is more beautiful, more fun, and more peaceful than anything we can imagine. He is preparing a **New Home** for us.

"He will wipe every tear from their eyes. There will be no more death or mourning or crying or pain, for the old order of things has passed away." (Revelation 21:4)

Think about your favorite day ever. Now, imagine a place where *every* day is even better than that one. In our New Home, all the "sad things" from Chapter 6 will be gone forever. No more boo-boos, no more mean words, no more getting sick, and no more saying goodbye. Everything that sin broke, God is going to fix.

What is Heaven Like?

People often ask, "Will I be bored in heaven? Will I just sit on a cloud and play a harp all day?" The answer is a big, loud **NO!** The Bible describes our future home as a "New Heaven and a New Earth." It won't be a floaty, ghostly place. It will be a real world with mountains, trees, water, and cities, except it will be perfect.

The Five "No-Mores" of the New Home:

1. **No More Darkness:** God's glory will be so bright we won't even need a sun or a moon.

2. **No More Fear:** You will feel 100% safe, 100% of the time.

3. **No More Sin:** No one will ever be mean, selfish, or dishonest again.

4. **No More Sadness:** Every "broken heart" will be totally healed.

5. **No More Separation:** We will be with God, seeing Him face-to-face!

Activity 1: The "Everything New" List

If you could pick three things from this world that you think God might make "even better" in the New Earth, what would they be? (Example: Puppies that never get old, fruit that tastes like candy, or being able to run without getting tired).

1. ____

2. ____

3. ____

The Great Reunion

The best part of a new home isn't the gold streets or the beautiful gates; it's the **people**.

When we get to our New Home, we will be reunited with all our brothers and sisters in Christ who have gone there before us. You'll get to meet David (the giant-slayer), Esther (the brave queen), and Peter (the fisherman). You will get to hear their stories in person!

But most importantly, you will be with **Jesus**. All the things we talked about in this book, His love, His grace, His power, you will get to experience while standing right next to Him. He is the one who built the home, and He is the one who makes it "Heaven."

Activity 2: A Letter to Future Me

Imagine you are already in the New Home, and you are looking back at the life you are living right now. What would you want to tell yourself about why it was worth it to follow Jesus?

*"Dear Me, Don't give up when things are hard, because __________

____

____

____

____

Being here with Jesus is _________________________________

____

____

____

____

Living with "Heaven Eyes"

Knowing that we have a perfect home waiting for us changes how we live today. It gives us **Hope**.

When a runner is in a race and their legs start to hurt, they don't stop. They look at the finish line and keep going. When you have a hard day at school or when things feel unfair, you can look at the "finish line" of Heaven.

- You can be **generous** today because you know you have riches waiting in Heaven.

- You can be **brave** today because you know God has already won the victory.

- You can be **patient** today because you know the "car ride" is almost over.

Home Lab: The "Telescope" Focus

This experiment shows how focusing on the future changes how we see the present.

What you need:

- A cardboard tube (from a paper towel roll).

- A small toy or picture placed at the other end of a long hallway.

What to do:

1. Look down the hallway normally. You can see the toy, but you also see the walls, the floor, the ceiling, and maybe some clutter.

2. Now, put the tube to your eye like a telescope and look *only* at the toy.

3. Everything else (the clutter and the walls) disappears from your view.

The Lesson: When we focus only on our problems (the clutter), we get overwhelmed. But when we use the "telescope" of faith to look at our New Home and the promise of Jesus, the problems don't seem so big anymore. We are focused on the prize!

Activity 3: The Welcome Home Drawing

The Bible says that in the New City, there is a "River of the Water of Life" and the "Tree of Life" with leaves that heal the nations. Draw a picture of what you think the entrance to your New Home might look like.

Write your favorite word to describe Heaven here:

Talk to God

"Dear Jesus, thank You for preparing a place for me. When I feel sad or scared, help me to remember that this world is not my final home. Thank You that one day there will be no more tears and no more pain. Help me to live with 'Heaven eyes' today, sharing Your hope with everyone I meet. I can't wait to see You face-to-face. Amen."

CONCLUSION
KEEP GROWING IN FAITH

Congratulations! You have officially reached the end of this book. We have traveled a long way together through these thirteen chapters. We started at the very beginning of time with **Creation**, explored the "Great Gap" caused by **Sin**, met our Hero and Savior, **Jesus**, and discovered how the **Holy Spirit** helps us walk through life every single day. We've looked at the importance of prayer, the beauty of the Church family, and the incredible promise of a New Home.

But here is a very important truth to hold onto: even though you have finished the last page of this workbook, you have not finished the story. In fact, you are just getting to the most exciting part!

Think of this book like a **training manual** for a deep-sea diver or a detailed map for a mountain explorer. Reading the manual is important because it teaches you how the equipment works and where the dangers might be. However, the real excitement doesn't start until the diver finally jumps into the sparkling blue ocean. The real fun begins when the explorer actually starts hiking up the trail, smelling the pine trees and seeing the view for themselves. This book was designed to give you the "tools" and the "map" you need, but the **adventure** of walking with God is something that happens out there, in your real life, every single day for the rest of your life.

The "Three-Legged Stool" of Growth

How do you keep your faith strong now that you've finished these lessons? Following Jesus is a bit like riding a bike or learning a new sport; if you stop practicing, you might feel a bit wobbly. To keep your faith from wobbling, it helps to focus on three main habits. Imagine a stool with three legs. If all three legs are strong, the stool is sturdy and you can sit on it safely. But if one leg is missing or broken, the stool will tip over. To keep your spiritual life sturdy, keep these three things in balance:

1. Keep Talking (Communication)

Don't let your conversation with God stop just because you finished the "Prayer" chapter. Remember, He is your Heavenly Father, and He never gets tired of hearing from you. Communication is the heartbeat of any relationship. If you stopped talking to your best friend, your friendship would eventually feel distant. It's the same with God. You don't need a formal "prayer closet" or a list of big words. Just talk to Him. Talk to Him about your breakfast, the math problem that is confusing you, and the things you are excited about for the weekend.

2. Keep Eating (The Bible)

Just like your physical body needs healthy food to grow taller and stronger, your spirit needs "God's Word" to stay healthy. The Bible is often called "Spiritual Milk" or "Bread." You don't have to read ten chapters a day to be a "good Christian." Instead, try to find one verse or one story each day. Read it slowly. Think about it while you brush your teeth. Ask the Holy Spirit, "God, what are You trying to tell me in this verse today?"

3. Keep Walking (Action)

Faith isn't just something we *know* in our heads; it's something we *do* with our lives. James, a writer in the Bible, said that faith without action is like a body without breath—it isn't really alive! When the Holy

Spirit gives you a "nudge" to be kind to someone who is lonely, or to tell the truth even when it might get you in trouble, follow that nudge! Every time you choose God's way over your own way, your "faith muscles" get a little bit stronger.

Understanding the Seasons of Growth

In nature, trees don't grow at the exact same speed every single day. In the spring, they sprout beautiful green leaves and flowers. In the summer, they grow deep roots. In the autumn, they might lose their leaves, and in the winter, they look like they are sleeping. But even in the winter, the tree is still alive, and its roots are still there.

Your life with God will have seasons, too.

- **Spring Seasons:** Sometimes everything feels new and exciting. You feel very close to God, and reading the Bible feels easy and fun.

- **Winter Seasons:** Sometimes you might feel a little bored, or God might feel far away. You might have questions that are hard to answer, or you might go through a sad time.

The most important thing to remember is that **God is with you in every season.** Just because you don't "feel" like you are growing doesn't mean God has stopped working in you. Deep under the soil of your heart, He is still building your roots.

The Tool of Memory

One of the best ways to keep growing is to hide God's Word in your heart. In this book, we have looked at thirteen different **Focus Verses**. These aren't just sentences to read; they are like "Survival Gear" for your brain.

When you feel scared, you can remember: *"The Lord is my Shepherd."* When you feel like you aren't good enough, you can remember: *"By grace you have been saved."* When you feel alone, you can remember: *"I will never leave you."*

Activity: My Favorite Promise Look back through your favorite chapters. Choose one verse that you want to memorize so well that you could say it even if someone woke you up in the middle of the night. Write it in big, bold letters in the space below:

Now that you've reached the end, it's helpful to look back at the trail you've climbed. Take a moment to think about these questions:

1. **What was the most surprising thing you learned about God's character?**

    ----

2. **Which "Home Lab" experiment helped you understand a spiritual truth the best? Why?**

    ----

3. **What is one thing you used to be confused about that feels clearer now?**

    ----

4. Who is one person you can share these truths with? (A sibling,
    a friend, or a cousin?)

The Golden Rule of the Journey: Grace Over Perfection

As you move forward, there is one very important thing you must never forget: **God is not looking for you to be perfect.** If you think that growing in faith means you never make a mistake again, you will end up feeling very frustrated. We are all "works in progress." Imagine a construction site for a beautiful skyscraper. Some days there are piles of dirt everywhere. Some days it looks messy and unfinished. But the Architect has the blueprints, and He knows exactly what the building will look like when it's done.

You are God's "construction site."

- There will be days when you make great choices and reflect His glory perfectly.

- There will be days when you lose your temper, tell a lie, or act selfishly.

When you mess up, the enemy (sin) wants you to hide from God, just like Adam and Eve did in the garden. But God wants you to do the opposite. He wants you to run **to** Him. Because of Chapter 8 (Grace), you can always say, "Father, I messed up. Please forgive me and help me try again."

God isn't a mean judge waiting for you to fail so He can punish you. He is a loving Father who is cheering for you as you learn to walk. When a baby is learning to walk and they trip and fall, the parents don't get angry, they pick the baby up, give them a hug, and encourage them to take another step. That is exactly how God feels about you.

Staying Connected to the Team

Remember Chapter 10? You are part of a family. One of the biggest mistakes a Christian can make is trying to grow all by themselves. We are like the coals in the grill—we stay "on fire" when we are bunched together.

Make it a priority to stay connected to your church family.

- Listen to your teachers.

- Ask questions when you don't understand something.

- Find older Christians who can encourage you.

- Be a "helper" to younger kids who are just starting their journey.

When we walk together, the journey is much more fun and much less scary.

The Final Promise: He Finishes What He Starts

The Bible contains a beautiful promise in a book called Philippians. It says: *"He who began a good work in you will carry it on to completion until the day of Christ Jesus."*

This means that growing in faith isn't something you have to do all by yourself. God is the one who "began" the work in your heart. He is the one who gave you the desire to learn about Him. And He is the one who promises to "complete" it.

You don't have to worry if you are "strong enough" to stay a Christian for the rest of your life. You aren't holding onto God; He is holding onto you. And His grip is very, very strong.

The Adventure Awaits

You are a special creation. You have been rescued by the Savior. You are guided by the Holy Spirit. You are a child of the King. You have a home in Heaven.

Now, it's time to close this book and open your eyes to the world around you. Every person you meet is someone God loves. Every day you wake up is a chance to show His glory. Every challenge you face is a chance to trust His power.

Keep reading. Keep praying. Keep loving. The adventure is just beginning!

"Dear Heavenly Father, thank You for everything I have learned in these thirteen chapters. Thank You for being my Creator, my Shepherd, my Savior, and my King. As I finish this workbook, I ask that You would keep growing my faith every single day. Help me to remember Your promises when I am scared and Your grace when I make mistakes. Help me to be a light in this world and to show others how wonderful You are. I am so glad I belong to Your family. I love You, Lord. Amen."

APPENDIX A

THE ATTRIBUTES OF GOD

Imagine you have a pen pal. You have never met them in person, but they write you letters every week. In the letters, they tell you about themselves. They might say, *"I am tall,"* or *"I have red hair,"* or *"I am very good at math."* These descriptions are called **Attributes**. An attribute is simply a trait or a quality that makes a person who they are.

If you asked your best friend to list your attributes, they might say you are funny, fast, kind, or brown-eyed. But what if we asked the Bible to list **God's** attributes? What is God actually *like*?

Many people make the mistake of thinking God is just a "super-sized" version of a human. They think He is like a nice grandfather in the sky, or a superhero with a cape. But the Bible teaches us something very different. It teaches us **Theology Proper**, which is the study of God Himself. It tells us that God is not just "bigger" than us; He is a completely different kind of being. He is the Creator, and we are the creatures.

In this special section, we are going to explore **Ten Great Attributes of God**. Some of these are things God shares with us (like Love), and some are things that belong only to Him (like being All-Knowing).

Get ready to stretch your brain. These truths are huge. They are heavier than mountains and deeper than the ocean. But learning them is the most important thing you will ever do, because the more you know about who God is, the more you will trust Him, love Him, and worship Him.

1. God is Eternal (Infinite)

He has no beginning and no end.

Have you ever tried to think about "forever"? It hurts your brain a little bit, doesn't it? Everything we know in our world has a beginning and an end.

- You had a birthday (a beginning).
- Your shoes were made in a factory on a certain day.
- Even the sun and the stars had a moment when they were created.

But God is different. He is **Eternal**. This means He never had a birthday. There was never a time when God did not exist. Before the universe was made, before angels were created, and before time itself started ticking, God was there.

Imagine a long piece of string that represents time. It stretches from the past to the future. You are a tiny dot on that string. But God isn't on the string at all. He created the string! He stands outside of time. He sees the days of the dinosaurs, the day you were born, and the day looking 10,000 years into the future all at the same exact moment. He is the "Alpha and Omega," the Beginning and the End.

Why Does This Matter? Because God is Eternal, He is never in a rush. He is never "running out of time" to fix your problems. Also, because He has always existed, He is the only One who truly knows how the story of the world ends. You can trust Him with your future because He is already there!

> **The Verse:** "Before the mountains were born or you brought forth the whole world, from everlasting to everlasting you are God." (Psalm 90:2)

2. God is Immutable (Unchanging)

He never changes, grows, or improves.

Think about how much you have changed since you were a baby. You grew taller. You learned how to talk. You learned math. Maybe you used to like strained peas, but now you hate them. Humans are constantly changing. We change our minds, our moods, and our plans.

God is **Immutable**. That is a big theological word that means "He does not mutate" or change. God never grows "older." He never learns something new (because He already knows everything). He never gets stronger (because He is already all-powerful). And most importantly, He never changes His character.

God will never wake up on the "wrong side of the bed" and be grumpy with you. He will never decide that He doesn't love you anymore. He will never cancel a promise He made in the Bible. In a world where everything changes, your friends, your school, your feelings, God is like a giant, unmovable Rock. He is the same yesterday, today, and forever.

Why Does This Matter? If God changed, we couldn't trust Him. Imagine if God was kind on Monday but mean on Tuesday! You would be scared to pray. But because He is Immutable, you know exactly who He is every single time you talk to Him. You can build your life on Him because He will never shift under your feet.

> **The Verse:** *"I the Lord do not change. So you, the descendants of Jacob, are not destroyed." (Malachi 3:6)*

3. God is Omnipresent (Everywhere)

He is present everywhere, all the time.

"Omni" is a Latin word that means "All." So, "Omnipresent" means "All-Present."

As a human, you can only be in one place at a time. If you are at school, you can't be at home. If you are in your bedroom, you can't be in the kitchen. But God is **Spirit**, which means He doesn't have a physical body that limits Him to one spot.

God is fully present in this room with you right now. But at this exact same second, He is fully present on the other side of the world in

Australia, and He is fully present on the moon, and He is fully present in a galaxy a billion light-years away. He isn't "stretched out" like a thin layer of butter over bread. He is *fully* everywhere.

This means you can never run away from God. In the Bible, a man named Jonah tried to run away on a boat, but God was there. David wrote that even if he made his bed in the deepest ocean, God would be there.

Why Does This Matter? For a person who is disobeying God, this is a scary thought—you can't hide! But for a child of God, this is the most comforting thought in the world. It means you are never alone.

- When you walk into a new classroom and feel scared... God is there.
- When you are lying in bed in the dark... God is there.
- When you feel lonely... God is right beside you.

    The Verse: *"Where can I go from Your Spirit? Where can I flee from Your presence?" (Psalm 139:7)*

4. God is Omniscient (All-Knowing)

He knows everything: past, present, and future.

How much do you know? You probably know your multiplication tables, the names of your friends, and the rules of your favorite video game. But do you know how many stars are in the sky? Do you know what your friend is thinking right now? Do you know what will happen next Tuesday? No, of course not.

God is **Omniscient**. He knows *everything* that can be known.

- **He knows the Universe:** He counts the stars and calls them all by name (Psalm 147:4).
- **He knows the Future:** He knows exactly what is going to happen a thousand years from now.
- **He knows YOU:** He knows how many hairs are on your head. He knows what you are going to say before you even open your mouth. He knows your secrets, your fears, and your dreams.

God never has to "learn" anything. He never Googles an answer. He never says, "Oops, I didn't see that coming!" He is the expert on everything.

Why Does This Matter? Sometimes we think we know better than God. We think, *"I want this toy right now!"* or *"I want to do things my way!"* But because God is Omniscient, He sees the whole picture. If He says "No" to something, it's because He knows something you don't. Trusting an All-Knowing God means believing that His plan is smarter than our plan.

> **The Verse:** *"Great is our Lord and mighty in power; his understanding has no limit." (Psalm 147:5)*

5. God is Omnipotent (All-Powerful)

He can do anything that fits with His character.

Think of the strongest thing you can imagine. A hurricane? A nuclear explosion? The gravity of a black hole? Compared to God, all of those things are weaker than a tiny candlelight.

God is **Omnipotent**. He has unlimited power.

- He spoke, and the universe appeared out of nothing.
- He holds the planets in orbit with just the "word of His power."
- He can split seas, heal the sick, raise the dead, and calm storms.

There is no rock too heavy for Him to lift. There is no problem too hard for Him to solve. Satan is not God's equal; Satan is a created being. God could stop Satan with a single breath if He wanted to.

However, there are things God *cannot* do. He cannot lie. He cannot sin. He cannot stop being God. This isn't because He is weak; it's because He is perfect. He cannot do anything that goes against His own good nature.

Why Does This Matter? When we face big problems—like sickness or scary news—we can feel small and helpless. But our Father is the Strongest Being in Existence. Praying to an Omnipotent God means knowing that He is able to handle whatever you give Him. As the angel told Mary, *"For nothing will be impossible with God."*

> **The Verse:** *"Ah, Sovereign Lord, you have made the heavens and the earth by your great power and outstretched arm. Nothing is too hard for you." (Jeremiah 32:17)*

6. God is Holy (Set Apart)

He is perfect and totally separate from sin.

The word **Holy** is the only attribute of God that is repeated three times in a row in the Bible: *"Holy, Holy, Holy."* In Hebrew culture, repeating something meant it was incredibly important.

To be Holy means two things:

1. **Unique:** God is in a class by Himself. He is "set apart" from creation. It's like comparing a diamond to a pile of mud. The diamond is special, rare, and pure.

2. **Pure:** God has absolutely no darkness in Him. He never has a bad thought. He never makes a mistake. He is blindingly, perfectly good.

Imagine looking directly at the sun. It is so bright and powerful that it hurts your eyes. That is a little bit like God's holiness. In the Bible, when people saw a glimpse of God's holiness, they fell down on their faces because they realized how small and sinful they were in comparison.

Why Does This Matter? Because God is Holy, He cannot be friends with sin. This is the bad news: our sin separates us from Him. But this is also why the Cross is so amazing. Jesus (the Holy One) took our sin so that we could be made holy and come close to God again. God's holiness reminds us that we should treat Him with respect and awe, not like a buddy we can ignore.

> **The Verse:** *"Holy, holy, holy is the Lord Almighty; the whole earth is full of his glory." (Isaiah 6:3)*

7. God is Sovereign (King)

He has absolute authority and control over everything.

Who is in charge of your life? Your parents? Your teachers? The President? While those people have some authority, God has **Ultimate Authority**.

Sovereignty means that God is the King of Kings. He sits on the throne of the universe, and nothing happens without His permission.

- The wind blows where He tells it to.

- Kings and rulers only rise to power because He allows it.

- Even the bad things that happen are under His control, and He can turn them around for good.

Think of a chess master playing a game. Even if his opponent makes a crazy move, the master knows exactly how to counter it to win the game. God is the ultimate Master. Even when the world looks chaotic, God is never panicked. He is always in control, working out His plan perfectly.

Why Does This Matter? The world can be a scary place. There are wars, sicknesses, and accidents. If no one was in charge, that would be terrifying. But because God is Sovereign, we can relax. We know that the One driving the bus is good, wise, and powerful. We don't have to worry about the future because the King is already there.

The Verse: *"The Lord has established his throne in heaven, and his kingdom rules over all." (Psalm 103:19)*

8. God is Just (Righteous)

He always does what is right and punishes evil.

Have you ever seen a bully get away with being mean and thought, *"That's not fair!"*? We all have a sense of justice inside us. We want good to be rewarded and bad to be punished. Where did we get that feeling? We got it from our Creator.

God is the Perfect Judge. He is **Just**. This means He never cheats. He never plays favorites. He never accepts a bribe. He always does exactly what is right.

This is a scary attribute because it means God cannot just "wink" at our sin. If a human judge let a criminal go free just because he felt like it, he would be a corrupt judge. Because God is a good Judge, He must punish sin. This is why the world has consequences for bad actions.

Why Does This Matter? If God wasn't Just, there would be no hope for the world. The bad guys would win. But because God is Just, we know that one day, He will fix everything. He will punish every evil deed and wipe away every tear. It also makes us thankful for Jesus. On the Cross, God's Justice and God's Love met. Jesus took the punishment (Justice) so we could have the forgiveness (Mercy). God remained Just, but He also became our Savior.

> **The Verse:** *"He is the Rock, his works are perfect, and all his ways are just. A faithful God who does no wrong, upright and just is he."* (Deuteronomy 32:4)

9. God is Love (Benevolent)

He gives of Himself for the good of others.

This is probably the most famous attribute of God, but it is often misunderstood. When the Bible says **"God is Love,"** it doesn't mean God is a fuzzy feeling. It means that at His very core, God is a Giver.

Even before the world was created, the Father, the Son, and the Holy Spirit loved each other perfectly. God didn't create us because He was lonely. He created us because His love is so big that it bubbled over! He wanted to share His joy with us.

God's love is not like human love.

- **Human Love** often says: "I love you *because* you are cute, or smart, or nice to me."
- **God's Love (Agape)** says: "I love you *even though* you are sinful, messy, and broken."

God didn't wait for you to clean yourself up before He loved you. As Romans 5:8 says, *"While we were still sinners, Christ died for us."* His love is an action, not just an emotion.

Why Does This Matter? You might feel unlovable sometimes. You might think, *"If people knew what I did, they wouldn't like me."* But God knows everything (Omniscience) and He still loves you completely. You don't have to earn His love by being good, and you can't lose His love by making a mistake. You are secure in His love forever.

> **The Verse:** *"And so we know and rely on the love God has for us. God is love. Whoever lives in love lives in God, and God in them."* (1 John 4:16)

10. God is Faithful (True)

He always keeps His promises and never lies.

Have you ever had a friend promise to come to your party, but then they didn't show up? It hurts when people break their word. Sometimes people lie on purpose, but sometimes they just forget, or something comes up that they can't control.

God is **Faithful**. He is the ultimate Truth-Teller.

1. **He Cannot Lie:** It is impossible for God to deceive you. If He says it in the Bible, it is true.

2. **He Cannot Fail:** Nothing can stop Him from keeping His promise. No traffic jam, no sickness, no enemy can prevent God from doing what He said He would do.

The Bible is full of thousands of promises. God promised Noah he would be safe in the Ark. He promised Abraham a son. He promised to send a Savior. And He kept every single one. Because He was faithful in the past, we know He will be faithful in the future.

Why Does This Matter? Life is full of uncertainty. We don't know what will happen tomorrow. But we have a Faithful God who has promised, *"I will never leave you nor forsake you."* When you feel shaky, you can hold onto His promises like a handle on a subway train. He will not let go.

The Verse: *"Know therefore that the Lord your God is God; he is the faithful God, keeping his covenant of love to a thousand generations."* (Deuteronomy 7:9)

Summary: The God Who Is All These Things

Now, here is the most amazing thought of all: **God is all of these things at the exact same time.**

- He is not *sometimes* Just and *sometimes* Loving. He is fully Just and fully Loving at the same moment.

- He is not *sometimes* Powerful and *sometimes* Gentle. He is Omnipotent and Merciful at the same moment.

This is the God we worship. He is the Infinite, Unchanging, Everywhere-Present, All-Knowing, All-Powerful, Holy, Sovereign, Just, Loving, and Faithful King.

When you pray tonight, don't just picture a small, friendly figure. Picture this majestic God who holds the universe in His hands, and remember the miracle: **He knows your name, and He calls you His child.**

APPENDIX B
THE NAMES AND TITLES OF JESUS

In our modern world, names are often just labels. Your parents might have named you "Liam" or "Sophia" just because they liked the sound of it, or maybe because it was a family name. But in Bible times, a name was much more than a label. A name was a **description**. It told people who you were, what you were like, or what destiny God had planned for you.

- **Jacob** meant "Deceiver" (and he was tricky!).
- **Abraham** meant "Father of Many Nations" (and he was!).
- **Moses** meant "Drawn Out" (because he was pulled from the river).

When we come to Jesus, we find something amazing: He doesn't just have one name. Throughout the Bible, Jesus is given dozens of titles and names. Why? Because He is so wonderful and so complex that one name simply isn't enough to describe Him!

If you looked at a giant diamond, you would have to turn it over and over to see how the light sparkles from different angles. That is what we are going to do in this section. We are going to look at **Ten Great Titles of Jesus**. Each title is like a different angle of the diamond, showing us a different part of His mission, His power, and His love.

This study is called **Christology**. It answers the most important question anyone will ever ask you: *"Who is Jesus?"* Is He just a good teacher? Is He just a nice man who lived a long time ago? Or is He something far, far greater? Let's find out.

1. Jesus (The Savior)

The Name Above All Names

Let's start with the name you know best: **Jesus**. It's the name we use when we pray, sing, and read the Gospels. But did you know this name wasn't an accident? God the Father picked it out specifically. Before Jesus was even born, an angel appeared to Joseph and said, *"You are to give him the name Jesus, because he will save his people from their sins"* (Matthew 1:21).

In Hebrew, the name is **Yeshua** (Joshua), which translates to **"The Lord Saves."** Think about that for a moment. Every time Mary called Him for dinner, *"Jesus!"*, she was literally saying, *"The Lord Saves!"* His very name was a promise of what He came to do.

Many people in history have tried to save the world.

- Generals try to save people with armies.

- Doctors try to save people with medicine.

- Politicians try to save people with laws. But none of them could save us from our biggest problem: **Sin**. Only Jesus could do that. He didn't come just to be a "Helper" or a "Coach." He came to be a **Rescuer**. Imagine a lifeguard diving into stormy water to pull a drowning person out. That is what the name Jesus means. He dove into our messy world to pull us out of death.

Why Does This Matter? This name reminds us that we cannot save ourselves. If we could be "good enough" to get to heaven, we wouldn't need a Savior. The name Jesus keeps us humble, but it also gives us hope. No matter how big your mess is, His name is bigger. He is the Savior, not just the "Advisor."

The Verse: *"Salvation is found in no one else, for there is no other name under heaven given to mankind by which we must be saved." (Acts 4:12)*

2. Christ (The Anointed One)

The King God Promised

Many people think "Christ" is Jesus' last name, like "Smith" or "Johnson." But Christ isn't a name; it is a **Title**. It comes from the Greek word *Christos*, which translates the Hebrew word **Messiah**. Both words mean the same thing: **"The Anointed One."**

In the Old Testament, you didn't just get a crown when you became King; you got **anointed**. A prophet would take a horn filled with special, sweet-smelling oil and pour it over your head. This symbolized that God's Spirit was coming upon you to give you power and authority for a special job.

For thousands of years, the Jewish people waited for "The Messiah"—the Ultimate King who would be anointed not just with oil, but with the Spirit of God without limit. They waited and waited. When Peter finally said to Jesus, *"You are the Christ,"* he was saying, *"You are the One we have been waiting for! You are the true King!"*

Jesus holds three "Anointed" offices perfectly:

1. **Prophet:** He speaks God's words to us.
2. **Priest:** He connects us to God.
3. **King:** He rules over the world.

Why Does This Matter? Calling Him "Christ" means we are pledging allegiance to Him. It means we acknowledge that He is the Boss. We don't just admire Him; we obey Him. When you say "Jesus Christ," you are saying, "Jesus is my King."

The Verse: *"Simon Peter answered, 'You are the Messiah, the Son of the living God.'" (Matthew 16:16)*

3. The Word (The Logos)

God Speaking to Us

The Gospel of John starts with a very mysterious sentence: *"In the beginning was the Word, and the Word was with God, and the Word was*

God." Later, it says, *"The Word became flesh and made his dwelling among us."*

Who is "The Word"? It is Jesus! The Greek word used here is **Logos**. In ancient times, this word meant the "logic" or "reason" behind the universe. But John used it to mean something even more personal.

Think about what your words do. Your words take the invisible thoughts inside your head and make them audible so other people can understand them. If you don't speak, I can't know you.

- Jesus is **God's Voice**.
- God the Father is invisible; no one has ever seen Him. But Jesus is the "Word" that makes the invisible God visible.

If you want to know what God thinks, look at Jesus. If you want to know what God loves, look at Jesus. If you want to know how God feels about sin, look at Jesus. He is the perfect "explanation" of who God is. He is God speaking to humanity in a language we can finally understand: a human life.

Why Does This Matter? Sometimes we look at the sky and wonder, *"God, who are You? Are You angry? Are You far away?"* We don't have to guess! We have "The Word." Jesus shows us exactly who the Father is. If you have seen Jesus, you have seen the Father. He is the communication of God's heart to yours.

> **The Verse:** *"The Word became flesh and made his dwelling among us. We have seen his glory, the glory of the one and only Son." (John 1:14)*

4. The Lamb of God

The Perfect Sacrifice

This is one of the most tender, yet powerful titles of Jesus. When John the Baptist first saw Jesus coming toward him, he didn't shout, "Look! The Lion!" or "Look! The King!" He pointed and said, *"Look, the Lamb of God, who takes away the sin of the world!"*

To a modern kid, calling a strong man a "lamb" might sound like an insult. Lambs are fluffy, weak, and gentle. But to a Jewish person in Bible times, this title meant one thing: **Sacrifice.**

In the Old Testament, when someone sinned, they had to bring a lamb to the temple. The lamb had to be perfect, no spots, no sickness. The lamb would take the punishment for the person's sin. This happened millions of times over hundreds of years. But the blood of animal lambs couldn't truly wash away human sin; it was just a temporary covering. It was pointing forward to something better.

Jesus is the **Ultimate Lamb**.

- He lived a perfect life (no spots of sin).
- He went to the Cross willingly (silent like a lamb).
- He took the punishment for the *whole world*.

Because Jesus died as the Lamb, we don't have to sacrifice animals anymore. The price has been paid in full, once and for all.

Why Does This Matter? This title reminds us of how much our salvation cost. It wasn't free for Jesus. He had to lay down His life. It also reminds us that He is gentle. He didn't come to crush us; He came to die for us. When you feel guilty for something you did, remember the Lamb of God has already carried that sin away.

> **The Verse:** *"Worthy is the Lamb, who was slain, to receive power and wealth and wisdom and strength!" (Revelation 5:12)*

5. The Great High Priest

The Bridge Builder

In the Old Testament, the High Priest was a very important person. He was the only one allowed to go into the "Holy of Holies", the most special room in the temple where God's presence lived. Once a year, he would go in to represent the people to God. He was like a bridge between a Holy God and sinful people.

But human priests had problems.

1. They were sinful themselves, so they had to offer sacrifices for their own mistakes.
2. They eventually died, so you always needed a new one.

Jesus is our **Great High Priest**.

- **He is Sinless:** He doesn't need to apologize for Himself.
- **He is Eternal:** He never dies, so He is *always* there to represent us.
- **He is the Bridge:** He didn't just go into a temple made of stone; He went into Heaven itself!

Right now, at this very moment, Jesus is sitting next to God the Father. Do you know what He is doing? He is **Interceding** for you. That means He is talking to the Father on your behalf. When you pray, Jesus says, *"Father, hear them. They are with Me."* He is our advocate, our lawyer, and our representative.

Why Does This Matter? Sometimes we feel too ashamed to pray. We think, *"God doesn't want to hear from me."* But because Jesus is our High Priest, we can walk boldly into God's presence! We don't need a human priest or a special building to talk to God. We have a direct line through Jesus.

The Verse: *"Therefore he is able to save completely those who come to God through him, because he always lives to intercede for them."* (Hebrews 7:25)

6. The Alpha and Omega

The Beginning and The End

Alpha is the first letter of the Greek alphabet (like "A"). Omega is the last letter of the Greek alphabet (like "Z").

When Jesus calls Himself the **Alpha and Omega**, He is saying, *"I am the A and the Z, and every letter in between."* This is a title of **Authority** and **Eternity**.

- **He was there at the start:** Jesus wasn't created in the manger in Bethlehem. He was there when the universe was spoken into existence (Colossians 1:16). He is the Author of life.
- **He will be there at the finish:** When history ends, Jesus will be the one standing there. He is the Finisher of our faith.

Think of your life like a book. Jesus wrote the first sentence (He gave you life), and He will write the last sentence (He will welcome you home). He surrounds you completely. You are never outside of His care because He exists before your problems start and after your problems end.

Why Does This Matter? This gives us incredible peace. If Jesus is the Alpha, it means He started a good work in you. If He is the Omega, it means He will finish it. He isn't a quitter. He oversees all of history, from the dinosaurs to the space age to the end of time. Nothing catches Him by surprise.

The Verse: *"I am the Alpha and the Omega, the First and the Last, the Beginning and the End." (Revelation 22:13)*

7. The Good Shepherd

The Protector and Guide

In ancient Israel, being a shepherd wasn't a relaxing job where you sat in the grass and played the flute. It was dangerous, dirty, hard work. Shepherds had to fight off lions, bears, and wolves. They had to sleep in the cold to watch over the sheep. They had to guide the sheep to water in the desert.

Sheep are not very smart animals. They get lost easily. They can't defend themselves (they have no claws or sharp teeth). They are totally dependent on the shepherd.

Jesus said, **"I am the Good Shepherd."** He contrasted Himself with a "hired hand." A hired worker runs away when the wolf comes because he doesn't own the sheep; he just wants the paycheck. But the Good Shepherd stays. He fights for the sheep. Jesus said He would even *lay down His life* for the sheep.

As our Shepherd, Jesus does three things:

1. **Feeds Us:** He gives us His Word.
2. **Leads Us:** He guides us through life by His Spirit.
3. **Finds Us:** When we wander off into sin, He comes looking for us. He doesn't wait for us to come back; He chases us down with His love.

Why Does This Matter? We all get lost. We all make bad decisions. It is comforting to know that we have a Shepherd who is committed to keeping us safe. When you feel lonely or confused about what decision to make, you can pray, *"Shepherd, lead me."* He knows the way to green pastures.

8. The Light of the World

The One Who Chases Away Darkness

Imagine being in a cave, deep underground. It is pitch black. You can't see your hand in front of your face. You are terrified of falling into a hole or running into a rock. Then, suddenly, someone turns on a massive, bright flashlight. Instantly, everything changes. The fear goes away. You can see the path. You can see the danger.

Jesus said, **"I am the Light of the World."**

Our world can be a dark place. There is the darkness of **Sin** (people doing bad things). There is the darkness of **Ignorance** (people not knowing who God is). There is the darkness of **Hopelessness** (sadness and despair).

Jesus comes like a sunrise.

- He reveals the truth (so we don't stumble).
- He exposes sin (so we can clean it up).
- He brings warmth (healing our hearts).

Light has a very special property: **Darkness cannot defeat it.** You cannot shovel darkness into a room to get rid of the light. But you *can* bring a single candle into a dark room, and the darkness must flee. Jesus is the unconquerable Light.

Why Does This Matter? When you are confused or sad, you are in a "dark" place. Jesus promises that if you follow Him, you will *"never walk in darkness, but will have the light of life."* You don't have to stumble through life guessing what the meaning of everything is. Follow the Light, and you will see clearly.

The Verse: *"I am the light of the world. Whoever follows me will never walk in darkness, but will have the light of life." (John 8:12)*

9. The Bread of Life

The One Who Satisfies

The Deep Dive Everybody gets hungry. You can eat the biggest Thanksgiving dinner in the world, but give it five or six hours, and your stomach will growl again. Physical food keeps us alive, but it never satisfies us permanently.

Jesus used this fact to teach a huge lesson. After He miraculously fed 5,000 people with lunch, they wanted to make Him King just so He would keep giving them free food. Jesus told them, *"Do not work for food that spoils... I am the Bread of Life."*

He was saying that human souls have a "hunger," too. We are hungry for love, for meaning, and for purpose. People try to fill that hunger with all kinds of "junk food":

- Video games
- Popularity
- Money
- Success

But none of those things fill the empty spot inside. We always want more. Jesus is the only "food" that fills the hole in our hearts. When we know Him, our soul says, *"Ah, this is what I was missing."* He gives us life that lasts forever.

Why Does This Matter? Are you ever bored, even when you have lots of toys? Are you ever lonely, even when you are with friends? That is "soul hunger." It's your heart telling you that you need Jesus. Run to Him, and He will satisfy you in a way that nothing else can.

The Verse: *"Then Jesus declared, 'I am the bread of life. Whoever comes to me will never go hungry.'" (John 6:35)*

10. The King of Kings and Lord of Lords

The Final Victor

We end with the most majestic title of all. When Jesus came the first time, He was a humble baby in a manger. He was a suffering servant. He allowed men to arrest Him and kill Him.

But the Bible tells us that when Jesus comes *back*, He will look very different. The book of Revelation describes Him riding a white horse, with eyes like blazing fire and many crowns on His head. On His robe is written the name: **King of Kings and Lord of Lords**.

This is a title of **Absolute Supremacy**.

- There are many "kings" (presidents, rulers, authorities) on earth. Jesus is the King *over* them.
- There are many "lords" (bosses, leaders). Jesus is the Lord *over* them.

He isn't just a religious leader; He is the Ruler of the Cosmos. One day, every knee will bow and every tongue will confess that He is Lord. The baby in the manger is actually the CEO of the Universe.

Why Does This Matter? Sometimes it looks like the bad guys are winning. It looks like Jesus is weak or that people have forgotten Him. This title reminds us of the truth: Jesus is currently seated on the Throne. He has already won the war against sin and death. We are on the winning team! We can live with courage because our Big Brother is the King of everything.

> **The Verse:** *"On his robe and on his thigh he has this name written: King of kings and Lord of lords." (Revelation 19:16)*

APPENDIX C

THE ESSENTIALS OF TRUTH
(THE APOSTLES' CREED)

Have you ever seen a massive ship docked at a harbor? Even when the waves get choppy and the wind starts to howl, that giant ship doesn't float away. Why? Because it is held in place by a massive, heavy iron **anchor** that goes deep under the water and hooks into the solid ground.

As a Christian, your "ship" is your life, and the "ocean" is the world around you. Sometimes the world gets very confusing. You might hear different people saying different things about God. One person might say, *"God is just a force in nature,"* while another says, *"It doesn't matter what you believe as long as you are nice."* How do you know what the truth is? You need an anchor. For almost 2,000 years, Christians have used something called **The Apostles' Creed** as their anchor.

What is a "Creed"? The word "Creed" comes from the Latin word *Credo*, which simply means **"I believe."** A creed is a short summary of the most important "must-know" truths of the Bible. It isn't a replacement for the Bible, but it's like a "Cheat Sheet" that helps you remember the most important parts.

The Apostles' Creed is the oldest and most famous summary of the Christian faith. It is called the "Apostles'" creed not because the 12 apostles wrote it themselves, but because it contains the exact teaching that the apostles taught. It is divided into 12 "articles" or points. In this section, we are going to walk through each point like a detective, unlocking the **Systematic Theology** behind each sentence.

The Apostles' Creed

I believe in God, the Father almighty, creator of heaven and earth. I believe in Jesus Christ, his only Son, our Lord, who was conceived by the Holy Spirit and born of the virgin Mary. He suffered under Pontius Pilate, was crucified, died, and was buried; he descended to hell. The third day he rose again from the dead. He ascended to heaven and is seated at the right hand of God the Father almighty. From there he will come to judge the living and the dead. I believe in the Holy Spirit, the holy catholic church, the communion of saints, the forgiveness of sins, the resurrection of the body, and the life everlasting. Amen.

Article 1: "I believe in God, the Father almighty, creator of heaven and earth."

The Deep Dive (Theology Proper) We start with the most basic truth: God exists. But the Creed doesn't just say "God"; it calls Him **Father Almighty**. This tells us two things about His character.

1. **Father:** He is personal and loving. He isn't a cold "energy" in space. He is a Dad who cares for His children.
2. **Almighty:** He has all the power (*Omnipotence*).

The Creed also confirms that God is the **Creator**. This means the world isn't an accident. Every mountain, every molecule, and every galaxy was designed by Him. Because He made it, He owns it.

Workbook Challenge: Detective Work Look up **Genesis 1:1** and **Psalm 103:13**.

- Genesis 1:1 tells us God is: ___________________________________

  ____

- Psalm 103:13 tells us God is a: ___________________________

  ____

Think About It: If God is both your *Father* (Loving) and *Almighty* (Powerful), why should you never have to be afraid?

Article 2: "I believe in Jesus Christ, his only Son, our Lord..."

The Deep Dive (Christology) Now we move to the second person of the Trinity: Jesus. The Creed uses three specific titles here that define our **Christology**.

- **Jesus Christ:** As we learned in Appendix B, this means "The Savior" and "The Anointed King."

- **His Only Son:** This tells us that Jesus is the same "stuff" as God. Just like a baby puppy is a dog because its parents are dogs, Jesus is God because He is the Son of God. He is "One" with the Father.

- **Our Lord:** This means He is our Master. We don't just ask Him for help; we follow His orders.

Check for Understanding: If Jesus is the "Only Son," can there be other ways to get to God? (Circle one) **YES / NO**

Why?____

____

The Deep Dive (The Incarnation) This is one of the most mysterious parts of our faith. It describes the **Incarnation**—when God became a human.

- **Conceived by the Holy Spirit:** This means Jesus didn't have a human father. He is fully God.

- **Born of the Virgin Mary:** This means He was a real human baby who was born just like you. He is fully Man.

Jesus is the **God-Man**. He had to be a man so He could represent us and die in our place. He had to be God so His life would be worth enough to pay for *everyone's* sins.

Workbook Activity: The Two Natures of Jesus List two things Jesus did that showed He was **Human** and two things that showed He was **God**.

- Human: ____
- God: ____
- Human: ____
- God: ____

Article 4: "He suffered under Pontius Pilate, was crucified, died, and was buried..."

The Deep Dive (Atonement) The Creed mentions a real historical person: **Pontius Pilate**. He was the Roman governor. This is important because it reminds us that Jesus' death wasn't a fairy tale or a myth. It happened at a specific time, in a specific place, in front of witnesses.

Crucified, died, and was buried: This proves that Jesus really died. He didn't just faint or fall into a deep sleep. He went into the ground. He gave up His life completely to pay our "Sin Debt." This is called **Substitutionary Atonement**—He stood in our place.

Think About It: Why do you think the Creed mentions that Jesus was *buried*? ____

____

(Hint: It's to show that His death was 100% real. You don't bury someone who is still breathing!)

Article 5: "...he descended to hell. The third day he rose again from the dead."

The Deep Dive (The Resurrection) The phrase "descended to hell" can be confusing. It doesn't mean Jesus went to be punished by the devil. In the original language, it means He went to the "place of the dead" (Hades/Sheol). It means He experienced death to the very fullest.

But then comes the best part: **The third day He rose again.** This is the **Resurrection**.

- If Jesus stayed dead, He would just be a dead hero.
- Because He rose, He is a **Living King**.

The Resurrection is the "receipt" that proves God accepted Jesus' payment for our sins. It shows that Jesus is stronger than death and stronger than the grave.

Workbook Quiz: True or False?

1. Jesus rose from the dead only in spirit, not in His body. **T / F**
2. Jesus rose on the third day, just like He promised. **T / F**
3. The resurrection means death is defeated forever. **T / F**

Article 6: "He ascended to heaven and is seated at the right hand of God the Father almighty."

The Deep Dive (The Ascension) After spending 40 days with His friends after the Resurrection, Jesus went back up to Heaven. This is called the **Ascension**.

He is currently **seated at the right hand of God**. In the ancient world, the "right hand" was the place of highest honor and power. Imagine a king's throne room; the person at his right hand is the one who carries out all his plans. Jesus isn't just "resting" in Heaven; He is **Ruling**. He is governing the universe and listening to our prayers.

Faith at Work: How does it make you feel to know that your Savior is currently sitting in the highest place of power in the universe?

Article 7: "From there he will come to judge the living and the dead."

The Deep Dive (Eschatology) This part of Systematic Theology is called **Eschatology**—the study of last things. The Creed promises that history is going somewhere. Jesus is coming back!

When He returns, He will be the **Judge**. This sounds scary, but for a Christian, it is actually good news. It means that one day, all the bullying, all the lying, and all the unfair things in the world will be dealt with. Jesus will set everything right.

Think About It: If you are "in Christ" (covered by His grace), do you have to be afraid of the Judge? (Check one)

[ ] Yes, I'm still scared.

[ ] No, because my Judge is also my Savior who died for me.

Article 8: "I believe in the Holy Spirit..."

The Deep Dive (Pneumatology) This is **Pneumatology**—the study of the Spirit. The Creed doesn't say "I believe in a good feeling" or "I believe in an invisible force." It says, "I believe in the Holy Spirit."

The Holy Spirit is the third Person of the Trinity. He is just as much God as the Father and the Son. As we learned in Chapter 9, He is our Helper, our Teacher, and our Comforter. He is the one who lives inside us to help us say "No" to sin and "Yes" to God.

Fill in the Blank: In John 14:26, Jesus calls the Holy Spirit the

----

Article 9: "...the holy catholic church, the communion of saints..."

The Deep Dive (Ecclesiology) This article is about **Ecclesiology**—the study of the Church. You might see the word "catholic" and think it refers only to the Roman Catholic Church, but that isn't what it means here. The word "catholic" (with a small 'c') simply means **"Universal."** It means the Church is one giant family that includes every true believer in every country and every time period.

- **The Communion of Saints:** This means we are all connected. We share the same Father, the same Spirit, and the same Hope. We are never alone!

Workbook Activity: My Church Family List three things you can do to help the "Communion of Saints" in your own town.

1. --

2. --

3. --

The Deep Dive (Hamartiology & Soteriology) This is the heart of the Gospel! **Hamartiology** is the study of sin (the problem), and **Soteriology** is the study of salvation (the solution).

Because of what Jesus did on the Cross, our sins are not just "hidden"—they are **Forgiven**. This means God takes our "record" of bad things and wipes it completely clean. He doesn't hold our past against us. When we come to Him in faith, He sees us as "Justified" (Just-as-if-I'd never sinned).

Think About It: Imagine you had a chalkboard covered in 1,000 mistakes. Then, someone comes with a wet sponge and wipes it so clean that the board looks brand new.

- Who is the one with the sponge?

- How does it feel to know your board is clean?

Article 11: "...the resurrection of the body..."

The Deep Dive (Glorification) Some people think that when we die, we just become "ghosts" forever. But the Bible teaches something much more exciting: **The Resurrection of the Body**.

Just as Jesus rose from the dead in a real, physical body, one day He will raise us, too! Our "new" bodies will be like our old ones, but better.

- No more glasses.
- No more braces.
- No more wheelchairs.
- No more getting tired or sick.

God loves His creation so much that He isn't just going to save our "souls"—He is going to save our **bodies**, too.

Workbook Activity: Imagine Your New Body If you could describe your "Resurrection Body" in three words, what would they be?

1. ____

2. ____

3. ____

Article 12: "...and the life everlasting. Amen."

The Deep Dive (Eternal Life) The Creed ends where everything begins: **Everlasting Life**. This isn't just about living forever (everyone exists forever somewhere); it's about **Life with God**.

Eternal life starts the moment you trust Jesus, and it continues forever in the New Heaven and the New Earth. It is a life of joy, discovery, and friendship with the King of the Universe.

Amen: We end the Creed with "Amen." This isn't just a way to say "The End." It is a Hebrew word that means **"So be it"** or **"It is true!"** It's like putting a period at the end of a sentence or a seal on a letter. You are saying, *"I stake my life on these truths."*

Summary: Your Faith Foundation

You have just walked through the 12 pillars of Christian Theology! Whenever you feel confused or when someone tells you something about God that doesn't sound quite right, come back to the Creed.

- Is God the Father? **Yes.**
- Is Jesus the Son who died and rose? **Yes.**
- Is the Holy Spirit our Helper? **Yes.**
- Is there forgiveness and eternal life? **Yes!**

If you hold onto these 12 truths, your anchor will stay deep in the ground, and your ship will stay safe, no matter how big the waves get.

Workbook Final Check: Go back and read the entire Apostles' Creed out loud. As you read each line, think about the "Deep Dive" we just did.

Which of the 12 articles is most comforting to you today?

Why?

HERE'S ANOTHER BOOK BY JAMES NORTHWELL THAT YOU MIGHT LIKE

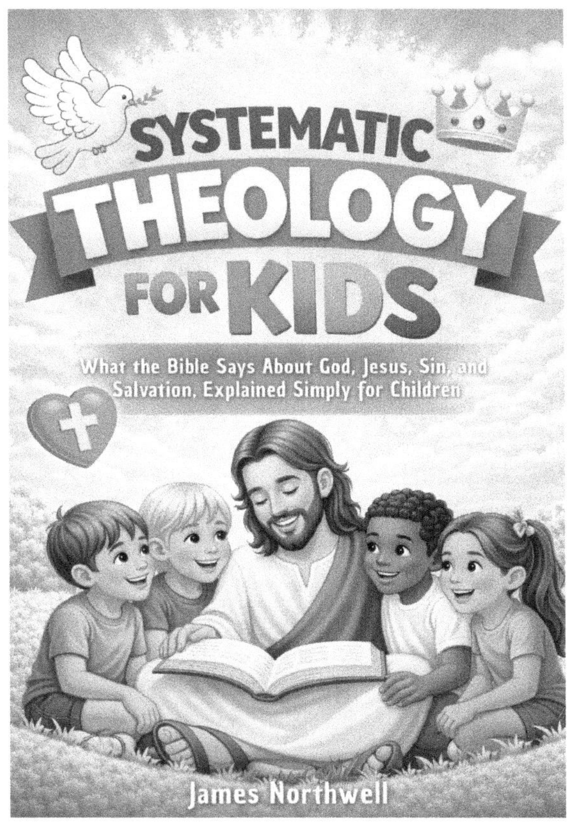